The Frugal Libertarian

Building Wealth in an Overspending World

Gregory Bresiger

Defiance Press & Publishing, LLC

DEFIANCE PRESS
& PUBLISHING

Published by:
Defiance Press & Publishing, LLC
www.defiancepress.com

ISBN:
eBook: 978-1-963102-90-1
Paperback: 978-1-963102-91-8
Printed in the United States of America

For permission requests or inquiries, contact Defiance Press & Publishing at: publishing@defiancepress.com

Dedication

For mis padres and the ever comely Suzanne Hall

Contents

Prologue

"Money is honey, Blum," Max Bialystok, in the movie "The Producers."

Money is sweet, but it can't solve all your problems. Still, money can be very important at some time in almost anyone's life.

Let me introduce you to the smart investor. He or she, young or old, can solve or survive many money problems and can also help others with basic money management skills, most of which are never taught in school.

This lack of knowledge can hurt millions of people. One is my former neighbor Judy. Who is Judy?

Judy is a friend. She is in her 60s and lives in an upper middle-class neighborhood in New York City. She is talented, speaks several languages---French is more like her first language---and has an important job at a private institute. She makes a middle-class income. She has had a good income for most of her life. So she should be secure in her golden years.

She isn't.

Judy, like millions of Americans today and probably millions more in the future, faces considerable money problems and can't retire. It didn't have to happen.

Recently, she asked me for advice because I was a business journalist for years. She thought that my experience could solve her problem, yet there is little I can do. I wish she had spoken to me twenty years ago.

What's wrong?

I asked how her retirement assets were invested and she told me, "I have no retirement assets."

What?

How does she propose to live the rest of her life? She told me that she had Social Security. On average, Social Security is paying about $19,000 a year or so. (It will be somewhat more next year owing to high rates of inflation, which automatically boosts the payments).

Yet she lives in one of the most expensive cities in the world. By the way, since city and state finances have been mismanaged, it is likely that rising taxes will make New York City even more expensive. I worry about Judy.

Another potential problem for Judy is this flawed government program called Social Security. It has gone through periodic crises and is facing another shortfall in the next decade or so owing to lawmakers kicking the can down the road: They, both Republicans and Democrats, have passed Social Security's problems to the next generation. The next generation is near. Problems could result in reduced payments in about a decade. More on this later.

For now, let's say that Social Security is important to you whether you are young or old, whether you understand it or not. If young and making a modest income, you will find, as I did in my 20s and 30s, that it is your biggest tax. It is an outrageously high tax when you are making a small salary. If elderly or approaching retirement, there is another potential problem.

One should be aware that Social Security has problems that

must be resolved by Congress and the president. These days they never seem in a mood to settle big picture problems because they are too busy cutting up each other.

What are the woes of America's crown jewel government retirement plan?

Social Security's trustees are warning that the program, unless something changes, will have to cut payments in the next decade or so.

The program has already had problems. What will happen this time?

Social Security changes have always meant lower payments and higher taxes. People are hurt whether they are paying into the system or receiving money from it.

That is what is going to happen again although most politicians are not going to seriously discuss these unpleasant subjects, especially in any election year. That's when our pols will overpromise almost anything to get your vote.

I tell Judy there are only a few things she can do, but that working a long time will be in her future. That is assuming that something like the Coronavirus doesn't take her job.

Protect Your Earnings

Judy's problem is her prime earning years are gone. If she had a regular savings plan in her 30s, 40s and 50s, if she had saved just a bit in her prime years---say 10 percent and some of that 10 percent could have been covered by tax breaks and employer retirement plan matches---she would likely have few money worries now. But she, along with millions of other Americans, didn't. They trusted the government would take care of them. That's a bad bet.

As a young man I knew many of these people. They were

people who, no matter how generous a retirement matching plan they had at work, insisted they couldn't take home one cent less than their entire pay. They never contributed to retirement plans at work or set up a retirement plan outside of work. That's even though IRAs have been available since the 1980s. The IRA, a qualified retirement account, usually contains tax breaks for those smart enough to use them.

A lot of young and middle-aged people are following this same Judy Road so please read on. I want to put all of my readers on a better road. (If you are in retirement and trying to manage your assets, there's also a chapter for you).

Judy didn't take the basic money management steps that could have helped. That's because no one explained the investment basics to her such as the wonders of compounding; how unexpected high rates of inflation can make life miserable even for people who think they are comfortable. These are some of the points we will explore.

By the way, why are there lots of Judys, many of whom are quite smart in other areas? It's because this kind of basic money education that will be explored isn't taught at most high schools or even universities. There, a lot of time is spent on political correctness, hate your country history and other idiotic courses that don't help anyone but build dependence on the welfare state. Most states don't even require one investment course in order to graduate from high school. Many young people get college degrees without learning anything about money management.

This is insane.

It is as ridiculous as living in a foreign country but insisting you won't learn a word of the language. For tens of millions of Americans money management is an obscure foreign language. They are handicapping themselves. Yet money management is at least as important as learning math, computer basics or a foreign language.

So now Judy can't get back those prime earning years. In achieving financial independence, as in so many other goals in life, start early. You're only young once.

That is why so many conscientious parents, worried about what is going on at many local public schools, are looking for alternative education options for their kids, whether it is charter or private or home-schooling. Their kids will only have one chance to get a good education. Time could run out on them as it has for Judy's goal of a comfortable retirement. As actor Mickey Rooney once wrote: Life is too short.

The same is true for your finances. You need to get going on achieving financial independence, or almost any other monetary goal, as soon as possible. Someday many of us could be Judys.

Getting Off the Road to Financial Disaster

This book is designed to ensure you don't miss that chance at financial independence that has been missed by millions of Judys. But it's worse: Tens of millions of would be Judys are on that same road.

My wife, Suzanne Hall, and I were far down the Judy Road some 35 years ago just after we were married. But we decided to take another road. We agreed on a few basic money steps. These were steps that seemed difficult at the beginning---indeed, back then sometimes we used to argue about money but now we never do---but soon we were used to them. Money was no longer stressful, and we became financially independent. These steps became as much a part of our lives as paying monthly bills or buying groceries on a daily basis.

What were they?

We agreed on responsible spending, regular saving and investing programs. We put in place automatic saving and investment techniques. Once we got used to them, we just started doing these things without thinking. They became a normal part of our lives. We didn't have to think about putting money aside each month for saving and investing. "Civilization," the philosopher Whitehead writes, "advances by the number of things we can do without thinking."

We stopped thinking about saving and investing. We just started doing.

How I Got Here

Part of why we got on that better road is in the middle of my career as a general news reporter/editor I switched from writing about pols---something I enjoyed as much as going to the circus as a kid and guffawing at the clowns---to writing about personal finance and advisors. That was a lucky break although I didn't realize it at the time. I started to learn more about the most effective saving and investing techniques. I wrote about them.

I spoke to and interviewed financial professionals. I wrote about their products and services. I took much of their advice and applied it to my life.

I ensured that my wife and I started saving and investing on a regular basis, with the goal of beating inflation. We adopted sensible spending practices. I will note some of them in these pages.

They are simple techniques that almost anyone can use, especially those who start with a round figure: zero. That's what we began with when we were married at the end of 1987, the year of the stock market crash.

I also took a series of second jobs to ensure we had enough

to invest. One of them was as a part-time ESL teacher. Sometimes students, many of them Hispanic and knowing I was a business journalist, would ask me questions about saving and investing. I preached the long forgotten Victorian gospel of thrift. I argued the idea so vigorously that one of my wonderful students dubbed me "El Mas Tacano de Todos" (The Stingiest of Them All").

I took the name not as an insult, but as praise. I was proud of my nickname. I urged my students to become Tacanos. These are people who are in control of their financial lives. They make few money mistakes. In baseball terms, they never throw to the wrong base and give away runs. They will not only prosper; they will be able to help others in a number of ways because they are financially independent. My wife and I today give much more money to charities because we're financially independent.

For the first time in my life my wife and I were in control of our finances. Before our marriage each of us had a checkered history. Both of us, as single people in our 20s and 30s, had missed rent checks; had lived from paycheck to paycheck; had almost nothing in assets.

Now we were headed in the right direction; the direction of being able to run our own lives and not worry about the next bill. We sold two apartments in New York City and have purchased an apartment in Shadyside in Pittsburgh.

Yet even before achieving financial independence in about twenty years, we enjoyed many things such as travelling and eating out but we did it in a responsible way. We did it in such a way that we could be confident that when the bills came due, we could pay them. We didn't have to worry about next month's credit card bills. This book is about how you can do the same, even though you're not earning a lot.

Indeed, I assume that you are like me. You make, made, or will make a middle-class income. You're not a corporate big shot or a star pulling in a six or seven-figure income. However, remember some of those people in high tax brackets also run into money woes. That's because many of them violated the principles here and ended up in financial hell.

I never made more than $90,000 a year even with multiple jobs and my wife also never made big bucks, yet we are comfortable today. While we did well with our investments, we weren't Warren Buffetts. Buffett makes returns of 20 percent a year, which makes him the Babe Ruth/Josh Gibson of investing. Our long-term stock average was about nine percent, which was fine because we often increased our monthly investment contributions as we could afford them.

How did we achieve financial independence on middle-class incomes and solid yet not spectacular investment returns?

Consistent saving, investing and rational spending are why we won the money game. It is a game lost by millions of Americans every day.

Why?

We have a culture, a tax code and an economic orthodoxy that preaches the opposite of what I teach here—run your finances like the U.S. government: Spend now and forget the consequences. By contrast, my wife and I rediscovered the values of our parents and grandparents.

Like me you might come from a small neighborhood or from any of the millions of small towns in America. Mine was a neighborhood in the South Bronx called Highbridge. Later it was a neighborhood in Queens called Woodhaven. This was an area right out of Archie Bunker's County. My wife's was a modest Pittsburgh neighborhood.

I want you to have what my wife and I have now achieved. But in trying to obtain almost any goal remember it is likely more difficult than you think: There are hurdles blocking even the most diligent. I will advise you how to avoid them or have them do the least damage. Let's examine some.

Chapter 1

Lots of People Want Your Property

They're after your property. They're after your earnings, dividends, capital gains, etc.

Indeed, from the first day you make money until the day you die, they're leering at your wealth.

Who? They are the wealth destroyers.

They are numerous.

They are all around you.

They could have a terrible effect on your life if you are not careful.

They, the wealth destroyers, are in no particular order the following: the government, some of your pushy, shameless relatives, the government, your personal needs, your wife, your husband, jealous neighbors, the government, credit card companies, pushy populist pols on the hustings with plans for bigger governments but little or no mention of how to pay for them, increasing health care costs as you age, the declining value of your dollars owing to the over creation of money with the resulting reduction of your buying power through inflation. All these wear on your wealth. And so does the government.

That's because, where your wealth is concerned, it never forgets you.

Dreams Becoming Nightmares

Each of the wealth destroyers will sap your wealth, aborting your efforts to create an independent lifestyle. They can destroy your plans for a house in a lovely suburban community, or an apartment in the center of the city or a lovely getaway somewhere that hasn't been overrun by traffic.

Do you want any or more of these things? Are you an average person who will earn a middle-class income over the course of a lifetime? Then what is your plan to build, protect and preserve wealth? In this age of ever higher taxation and runaway consumerism, everyone needs a plan to accumulate and protect wealth.

Looking for the Holy Grail? It Isn't Here

This book isn't the Holy Grail of wealth creation. I don't have the name of a hot stock that will make you a millionaire overnight.

I don't have a Hillary Clinton cattle futures tip for you. I also can't provide you and yours with the political pull to obtain tens of millions of dollars in tax breaks that someone like Donald Trump obtained in his years as a New York builder. However, I am someone who, along with my wife, started with almost nothing. Today, my wife, Suzanne Hall, and I are comfortable even though neither of us ever made big bucks. We are financially independent, even as markets crash from time to time because the country is in recession or near one.

My wife is a former airplane mechanic, now playwright. I am a business journalist who is anything but a household name. I never made it to big-time journalism, but I earned a decent living over some four decades.

Neither of us has ever made a ton of money. I never worked

for the big boys of the business. The best I could in the way of glamour was as a part-time business reporter for the New York Post Sunday Business section for some 19 years. I also worked for various other business publications such as Financial Advisor, Financial Planning and Traders Magazine as well as various web sites such as Mises.org, the Epoch Times, InsideSources, the New York Sun and the Future of Freedom Foundation. When you live in New York City, as we did for some 30 years, you need more than one income just to be middle class.

My wife, I am proud to say worked for Delta Airlines for some ten years as one of the first female mechanics at Kennedy Airport. It was her last full-time job. She has had some of her plays produced off-Broadway but, to date, neither of us has ever earned huge amounts and we started in 1987 with almost nothing.

So how did we achieve financial independence without ever earning a bundle; achieving the right to never have to ride the egregious E-train to Manhattan ever again?

We worked hard, spent sensibly, saved and invested consistently over a number of years—about 25 years—and had a saving, investing and spending plan that we followed in bad times as well as good. Our success is in part because of the knowledge that came my way. I have dealt with some brilliant people over the course of many years. By listening, observing and writing, I have learned some techniques of wealth creation and destruction. By the way, avoiding the latter is as important as doing the former. You win in life and personal finance by minimizing mistakes as well as doing smart things.

It is one of the themes of this book that it is just as important to protect your wealth as it is to amass it. In personal finance, playing defense is at least as important as playing offense (Maybe more; championship teams in almost any sport often have a defense first philosophy). Most of the techniques I recommend aren't rocket science. Most are based on common sense. But commonsense ideas, the same as basic principles of liberty, must be repeated from time to time, must be passed from one generation to another, or they are lost. Many struggling young people today, deep in card or student loan debt, are lost.

It is a time when credit card debt numbers and bankruptcies are at record levels because many people thought the government would take care of them, no matter their circumstances. (For instance, consider the millions who think that their student loans have been forgiven. Despite the promises of the Biden administration.).

Many Americans are also using credit card debt to pay monthly bills, a self-destructive practice that could lead to disaster. How does one avoid these problems?

This book is an accumulation of the wisdom of many people who I have met in decades in business journalism. It also contains various stories of how average people spent themselves into financial disaster. Yet many of these problems could have been avoided by following commonsense practices that I will outline.

I believe that these practices can help you, the average person, with a middle-class, or somewhat below middle-class, income arrive at a good place: I believe that one doesn't have to make a bundle to achieve financial independence. Someone with a middle-class income or even something less can reach this goal. However, you should be patient and follow the automatic saving, investing and spending techniques I will recommend. You will eventually take them for granted.

Why?

Achieving financial independence requires a commitment to a plan over years or decades. It is designed with younger people in mind. But middle-aged people can also benefit. Indeed, at the end of the book, I also offer ways for those who are retired with a decent amount of assets to ensure that they will reduce their chances of running out of money.

But it all begins with a commitment by you and your loved ones.

When my wife and I agreed to saving, investing and working toward financial independence we had almost nothing. We had lost a lot of time. We were already in our late 30s when we wed. But I think that the principles here can even help those in their 50s and 60s, although it is more difficult for them than someone with prime earnings years ahead.

Who Are You, Dear Reader?

Are you someone who has taken the first steps to achieving these goals that only substantial wealth can bring? Congratulations. But remember, despite any success you may have had, there are many ways that you can be tripped up. How? Please keep reading.

Chapter 2

Take Cover! The Wealth Destroyers Are Gunning for You

You must have a tax strategy.

Wealth can take years to build, yet it can be destroyed in a moment. Lots of people would ruin your life. Who are they?

They are money hungry governments, headed by career pols who say they only want to raise taxes on the rich. Always ask them: What do you mean by "rich" and what will be the secondary effects, the effect on the economy, of increased taxation on the well-heeled?

Probing our career politicians often one comes across an unpleasant truth: Sometimes what they mean by "rich" is people with upper middle-class incomes or even lower middle class. But these kinds of things aren't clarified in the heat of elections. Indeed, that's where vote hungry pols often make the most outrageous promises and later, after the election, will claim memory loss when questioned about these promises.

They Make the Promises—You and Your Children Pay the Bill

Let me stipulate that democratic governments, almost all of them, are run by career pols. Texas is one of the exceptions. In Texas, state legislators are part-time officials who earn their primary income in the private sector. Ninety-five percent of them work in the private sector, which is a smart way to run a state government.

Many Texas lawmakers own businesses. That is healthy; it can lead to a sharing of interests between the governors and the governed that we don't see in most governments state and federal today. Texas has no state income tax. Is it an accident that Texas has some of lowest taxes and highest growth rates in the country? I think not.

But most pols outside of Texas and a few other places have a ravenous appetite for wealth. That's because they almost always have plans to expand the government. Few of them ever think about how government wastes money or what it is like to work in the private sector or that it would be a good idea if a government finds ways to spend less money.

Many career pols have no more worked on a regular basis in the private sector than they have ridden public transit or sent their kids to public schools. They don't consider how their spending plans result in more debt, more taxes and a harder life for tens of millions of people, most of whom will never earn superstar salaries or enjoy the level of retirement benefits that our rulers award themselves.

Taxes, direct or indirect, will likely be the biggest impediment to your efforts to achieve financial independence. That's because most career pols will never even consider the effect of high tax rates on the economy and average people. They think that raising tax rates will just hurt the rich. Not true.

Indeed, as a U.S. Treasury secretary of the 1920s warned in his book, "Taxation: The Peoples' Business," high tax rates hurt everyone, even people with modest incomes. That's because some taxes are imbedded in the prices of the goods and services we use almost every day. Some of these taxes we see. But many others are invisible. They quietly drive up prices. This makes it more difficult for millions of Americans to pay their bills of daily living.

All this means these pols and their successors almost always want more of your money and that of your children and their children. So it is critical that we discuss ways of lowering some taxes.

Why are taxes so important today and will be tomorrow? Most popular welfare state governments, faced with money problems, will pretend they're only after the wealth of the rich and that they're the only ones who will pay more.

This is untrue. The math of bigger government is indisputable.

It is the middle class that is bloodied by the relentless expansion of government since we are in the majority. Why do these career politicians wreak havoc? Why do they hurt the people they say they want to help?

Part of the reason, I believe, is that more and more of our pols have never worked in the private sector, much less run a business. That's because in a typical advanced welfare state democracy, the first order of business of the career politician is to get elected and the second order is to get re- elected. But how does one succeed at politics, regardless of whether one is on the left or the right? By promising responsible spend and tax policies? By telling people hard truths that the previous governments they elected have saddled them and their scions with huge amounts of red ink.

No.

Winning elections means making huge, sometimes insane, promises about creating or expanding programs. Back in 1972, the president, Republican Richard Nixon, and a Congress controlled by the opposition Democratic party, were both running for re-election. They tried to outdo each other over which party could out-promise the other in raising Social Security benefits since the elderly were, and remain, a key voting block.

Many elderly people were delighted to receive higher Social Security benefit checks just before they went into the voting booths. They were so happy that they re-elected both the president and most Democrats in Congress. Before the election President Nixon and leaders in Congress argued over who deserved credit for the benefit hikes.

History Repeats

Does that remind you of anything?

In another presidential election year, 48 years later, President Trump and the Democrats in the U.S. House of Representatives, where all money bills originate, argued over who deserves credit for your paltry $1,200 stimulus check that most Americans received. That was money that was created out of thin air—the government didn't have trillions of surplus dollars—and which will help devalue our currency as deficits, debts and inflation rates continue to grow no matter who is in office.

The problem with the stimulus payments of 2020 and the Social Security increase of 1972 was that later the bills came due. Payroll taxes to pay for Social Security programs started soaring. Most pols, both left and right, didn't care. They won their elections—president Nixon carried 49 out of 50 states—and they moved on to other things.

Indeed, some pols when they retired moved on to Florida and started collecting government pensions that are better than the Social Security payments their constituents received. I wrote about this in "The Great Social Security Deal of 1972," which is available at Mises.org.

When I wrote this, presidential and Congressional elections were taking place. And, of course, many of the candidates were promising incredible "free" things from free college tuition to the expansion of other federal programs.

Remember, you may like some or all of these programs, but they're not "free." You and generations to come will pay for them. If you want something, buy it. But understand beforehand what it will cost you as a citizen who pays taxes, taxes and more taxes.

You and your relatives will be paying them for generations to come through direct taxes as well as inflation, which is now, once again, wrecking the American economy. Inflation is a stealth tax that increases more and more as the government expands the money supply at dangerous rates and the government runs up red ink.

The nation, as I write this, is somewhere north of some $36 trillion or so in debt. The number keeps going up as both major parties compete to see which one can "give" us the most. However, I believe this is also untrue. I believe the true number is much larger. Why am I suspicious? That's because the government is doing the counting and the government isn't going by generally accepted accounting principles (GAAP).

These are standards the government imposes on others, but not on itself. Indeed, I once wrote a story for the New York Post Sunday business section in which numerous economists, both left and right, agreed the official government debt number was a fraud. It was a lot more than the published figure. One even said the nation was "functionally bankrupt."

https://groups.google.com/g/bible-prophecy-news/c/y3 yyOKG2_8E

By that he meant that, if a large percentage of people suddenly wanted their money, the government couldn't pay them. (Our regulated banks operate on a similar system. It is called fractional reserve banking. Government debt is a mortgage on every taxpayer's future earnings and how the nation has faced economic hard times. It is also a mortgage on taxpayers yet to be born, whose interests are being ignored. One of the dangers of the modern welfare state is the economic interests of fetuses and children are not represented. In figuring your financial future you need to consider these unpleasant financial facts, which are the products of both major parties).

I wish I could say just ignore the political circuses and get on with your life, but it is important to understand why you can't. Everyone will need a lot more money to do anything from retire to putting a young person through college as the value of money declines. It is inevitable that future governments, both left and right, are going to take much more from citizens.

There are few politicians left or right who have made it their life's work to cut down on spending and programs. So don't expect to hear that too often at the hustings. Elections are events in which pols, seeking to buy another term or get elected for the first time, won't mention the costs of their promises, or grossly underestimate them. Often they tell you that only billionaires will pay more taxes and the rest of us will pay less, which is risible.

Pols make promises to win elections. For example, in a glowing endorsement of Hillary Clinton for president in 2016, even the New York Times wrote this of her and her many promises of new or expanded government programs: "Mrs. Clinton and her team have produced detailed proposals on crime, policing and race relations, debt-free college and small-business incentives, climate change and affordable broadband. Most of these proposals would benefit from further elaboration on how to pay for them, beyond taxing the wealthiest Americans."

Exactly.

Promises, Promises

There was no way Ms. Clinton could have ever kept all her promises by just taxing the richest of the rich. In almost any modern welfare democracy there are never enough rich people to go around; to pay all the bills of an ever-expanding state.

Mind you, "The Times" said these things while endorsing Clinton! She went on to stunning defeat in part because many Americans didn't trust her promises of bigger government with only a select group of the well-heeled footing the bill for her incredible promises. Hillary Clinton once wrote she "likes to think big." Most politicians are the same.

Candidate Donald Trump, in 2016, complained about the deficits of the previous years, especially the trillion-dollar deficits of the first Obama years. That's when the nation was in recession. But the Trump presidency got better growth rates but still had a lot of red ink. President Biden went further in running up red ink.

What does that tell you?

Governments, left and right in the modern welfare state democracy, share one characteristic—they overspend. They spend with a reckless disregard and pass on the bills to generations unborn. Your taxes were and will continue to rise no matter who is in office.

Remember why you will need more in assets, much more than you think, to be comfortable: Political promises are paid for in one way or another either through taxes or money printing and inflation. Those things will squeeze you in retirement. They will squeeze you in middle age. They will squeeze your children as they start out in the workplace. So whether young or old, you should overprepare and be ready for broken promises.

For example, the promises of 1972 led to red ink in the Social Security system. Of course, years later Social Security taxes had to be raised. I remember, as a young man in my 20s and 30s, not making a lot of money but looking at the Social Security tax part of my pay stub—the FICA part—and thinking, "This FICA must be a huge pig." Yet, despite all this extra tax money, over the years, Social Security benefits have been cut, sometimes in subtle ways.

Here's an example: At one time, you never paid taxes on your Social Security payments. Why should you? By the time you receive Social Security, you will have paid into the system for generations. For example, I started working at age 16 and didn't collect Social Security until I turned 70. That's 54 years of paying these egregiously expensive payroll taxes, which were a hardship in my early years of work when I made little.

Paying taxes on your Social Security payments constitutes double taxation but that never stops our hired help, whether left or right, from inventing new forms of double and triple taxation. They depend on the average voter forgetting their promises.

Inflation is a more subtle, but no less destructive tax that affects almost everyone. But most people don't understand how it happens so they won't become angry with our spendthrift political ruling classes of both parties and the mainstream media that often enables them.

Too much spending leads to persistent cycles of more and more taxes along with high inflation rates---a kind of backdoor tax---until taxes can become almost unbearable. Then, too late, almost everyone starts to understand what inflation does to us as the value of the currency deteriorates at a shocking pace.

But fortunately for governments looking to raise taxes and con people with the promise of more "free" services, not a lot of Americans study history

This book offers various strategies to cope with numerous forms of taxation. Why do you need them?

The never-ending government spending combined with taxation, along with a rampant culture of "I've got to have it now consumerism," have ruined many a life. Many who once seemed prosperous, now have broken financial lives.

The Magnificent Bankrupts

Yet, at some point, most of these people made money—sometimes very good money—and often for decades. They were people we once envied.

Still, they ended up with nothing or just eking out an existence in the last years of their lives. "The Magnificent Ambersons" ended up in the same place as famous talk show second banana Ed McMahon—a man who likely made $100 million or more in his career. They ended up broke. If when I was a young man in the 1970s and 1980s someone had told me that the ultra successful McMahon would end up hard up for money, I would have not believed it.

Money woes would have been something that would have been inconceivable to the McMahons and the Ambersons throughout most of their seemingly blessed lives. Yet tens of millions of people in advanced welfare states in America and Europe, people who make good incomes through most of their lives, are following this same sorry path.

I don't want you to suffer money ulcers. I want you to achieve many or most of your dreams.

I want your years—young, middle and last—to be years in which you may not have everything—it would be boring to have everything. What would there be to shoot for? I want your years to be ones in which you and your family can live comfortably, feeling confident in your financial future.

We're not Mashuggah

Yet this book will offer you no crazy overnight dreams of wealth. These are the kind of dreams pursued by poor souls whose primary wealth creation strategy is throwing away ten or twenty dollars or more a week playing the lottery. By the way, the latter is a rigged game in which the odds of winning a substantial prize are never advertised for obvious reasons. It is no different than the numbers rackets that were run by organized crime until governments elbowed them out of the way.

But how can these commonsense approaches make your life better?

First, before a person can come up with a wealth generating strategy, one must recognize the numerous ways that wealth can be stillborn. To get from point A—a young person with little or nothing or a middle-aged person with a small amount of assets who wants more or an elderly person who has accumulated a stake, but who could lose it—to Point B, financial stability, or perhaps independence, requires a plan. A good plan in anything always assumes that something could go wrong. Then what?

In this book, we will discuss effective financial strategies for accumulating wealth and holding on to it over the long term. We will assume that many bad things can happen to you in your efforts to reach financial independence. Our topics include saving, investing, spending, how to use cash and credit cards, among others. We also review common traps that can destroy your portfolio, bank account or retirement account.

Look Out for Those Traps

These traps will stop you from sending your child to a first-rate university. They will prevent you from ever starting a business. And a small business is one of the most common ways that people improve themselves; making a better life for their families and, possibly, leaving something of value to the next generation. You must be proactive in avoiding these traps that would destroy your efforts to achieve financial independence.

Again, step one is to recognize that there are many ways your dream can become a nightmare. Remember, the wealth destroyers are just waiting to take hard earned money from you and a lot of them are public officials who claim to be serving you.

Yet the political ruling class, both left and right, seems to exist to perpetuate themselves. They grow bigger and more powerful by gathering more money. Most governments don't care if you succeed or not. They care that you have wealth that they can tax and tax some more, which is an anomaly.

The anomaly is governments want more and more money for their expanding welfare states, but often seem not to care how they hurt the men and women who create wealth. They are people who work two or three jobs to make ends meet such as my saintly father. They are often small business people who devote their lives to building an economic entity that serves the community or those who save and invest regularly, the same as most of our grandparents, whose shoulders we are standing on today. These people are the economy, yet government policies often destroy them. This makes about as much sense as working a golden goose to death because it isn't laying as many eggs to satisfy your endless appetite.

But the wealth destroyers often are aided and abetted by incendiary work of someone you would never guess. Many times that person is you. Many people, like the Ambersons and the Ed McMahons, spend themselves into a lower standard of living, poverty or, in increasing numbers in America, bankruptcy.

So first let's examine how you spend. Let's look at your consumerism. Here are critical factors in determining if you can create and sustain the wealth that will make life better for you and your family.

Chapter 3

Consumerism, Smart and Dumb

"Dear, BrandX Loan Company, we have no equity left in our house, can we still refinance our home?"

"No money down. Just sign and drive it!!! "Call now!" [Frequent radio and television commercials imploring us to spend Immediately]

"You gotta be in it to win it!" "Hey, you never know". [Part of radio ads for the New York State Lottery]

BrandX Loans' big shots want you to buy their product in the worst way.

So BrandX Loans thinks that some people with little or no equity in their homes can still get more credit. They can go still deeper into the red. But BrandX Loans and others getting you to make needless purchases aren't considering how this may affect your long-term wealth creation or how it could push you into bankruptcy.

You must do that for yourself.

However, former New York Giants football player Carl Banks, pitching cars on the radio, concludes his commercial for Kia Motors by asking, "Why wait?" But he hasn't a clue what a three year or four-year credit car buying plan will do to your finances. Still, he wants you to buy now.

Sign it and drive it is a phrase I often hear. What it means is that you are buying a car with no or a small down payment, or 100% on credit. That means you pay a great deal in finance charges for a set of wheels. But no one mentions that in the ad. The car dealer is more interested in moving the merchandise. The person trying to sell you the car is not thinking if the car purchase will compromise your ability to save and invest.

Pols to Americans: Run Up Some More Debts

Those politicians who want you to play the lottery, and never want you to know the almost impossible odds of winning a prize, don't think about the long-term effect on your wealth of spending $10 to $15 a week on lottery tickets.

For more on that see my article "The Lottery Racket" at Mises.com. "One's chance of winning a top prize in one of the rigged state lotteries is so close to zero as to be indistinguishable from zero.

https://mises.org/library/lottery-racket

Those annoying tube announcers who conclude ads with a frenzied demand to "call now," also have no idea what buying their products will do to your budget. They can all help you get deeper into debt. That is, if you help them achieve their sales goals at the expense of your financial health.

Why make Carl Banks, Brand X Loans, pols pushing lotteries, other well-heeled individuals and businesses wealthy at your expense? I assure you that none of these people will bail you out when you can't pay your bills. They don't go to bed thinking about whether people who buy their products and swallow the malarkey about lotteries are going into debt.

It is your responsibility to identify the con artists, legal and illegal, and pushy salesmen and steer clear of them. You are the person who should know best about your finances and how red ink can destroy them. You are the CEO of your life.

You Don't Need to Have Everything Today

Mindless debt, which is often the result of the desire to have more and more things right now even though one already has a lot, is ruining tens of millions of lives. That's not an exaggeration. Think of the millions of families whose lives have been ruined because no one understood basic money management.

Still, these are often people with good incomes or who once had good incomes. They are people who might have been wealth creators and achieved lifetime financial independence, if they had put automatic spending, saving and debt controls in place in the prime earning years of their lives. They never learned the lessons. They had no one to educate them. They missed their chance and some will never have that chance again.

It is ironic that so many people, along with many of their governments with big fat economies to tax, have so much debt. The irony is America, once the wealthiest nation in the history of the planet, with the highest standard of living in history, has a government on the road to bankruptcy as are many of its citizens.

Who Needs to Save?

Part of the problem of why so many people are deep in debt is a tax code and a culture that demean saving or investment, or what some call production. Instead, our culture and tax policy celebrate demand or consumption. We have economists who defend these policies. Indeed, the most famous, praised, economist of our time is still John Maynard Keynes, who died around the end of World War II, but his influence goes on and on. He justified government deficits as a way of ensuring permanent prosperity. Politicians in welfare democracies loved that idea, thinking it justified their reckless spending.

The greater economist is the little-known friend of liberty, Ludwig von Mises. Mises believed high standards of living are built through saving and investment over generations; that the high standard of living any society enjoys is built by generations of our economically literate, disciplined grandparents and parents.

Mises was an Austrian economist who was targeted in his lifetime by both the Communists and the Nazis. He championed saving and predicted the failure of the Soviet Union in the 1920s because it rejected markets. Mises was ridiculed by many for saying that. Back then millions in the West were hailing the Soviet Union as the wave of a wonderful future. They were calling for Western nations to adopt many its planning techniques.

Even as late as the 1970s and 1980s well known and respected economists, such as Paul Samuelson and John Kenneth Galbraith, were paying tribute to the "accomplishments" of the Soviet Union. It was a strange, cruel, socialist nation that imploded in the early 1990s.

What were its failures? There were many. But let's note one: It was a country with much of the most fertile land on earth, yet it couldn't feed its own people. It had to buy grains from capitalist nations.

Most of our career pols worship Keynes's ideas even if they have never read a word of his dense books.

Why?

His ideas, even dimly understood, give them license to do what they love to do: spend and spend some more. These ideas are communicated to many of their constituents. They start running their personal lives in the same fashion as the government runs its finances. These pols should be concerned with the state of the economy and with the tens of millions of people headed for financial problems over the next few decades.

Yet few of our pols are concerned about anything but winning the next election. However, who will pay the taxes when millions of us have little or nothing in assets and have declining income? Why do these leaders pursue reckless policies that seem good today and blow up later? It's all about power.

The Perpetual Campaign

Politics is about the short term, the next election, not the long term. Most career pols, both left and right, are too busy thinking about the next political campaign to give serious study to economies, how to create strong ones over the next generation and how to help individuals with no financial assets get some. They downplay the benefits of saving, investing and production.

They penalize success and those who would improve themselves. They say they are only aiming at making the rich pay more. But their policies end up hurting the rest of us. I give one personal example.

While working for a small publishing firm in New York back in the 1980s, I received a year-end bonus for one of the few times in my life. It was $2,000. That was a hell of a lot of money for me then. My wife Suzanne was delighted. Our annual household income at that time was only about $35,000. An extra two thousand dollars was a lot of money.

But, because it was a bonus, it was taxed at a 60 percent rate. That was far above our income tax bracket. I wasn't an investment banker getting a $2 million bonus each year, I was just a middle-class business writer. However, I was taxed as though I was making billion-dollar deals on Wall Street.

My wife and I were disgusted. I only brought home $800. They tax capital gains. They tax savings. The predictable result is that America has some of the lowest savings' rates in the West and that there is a big retirement savings shortfall. (Both on the part of individuals not saving enough for their golden years and a Social Security program that lacks sufficient reserves, which will be forced to reduce payments in about a decade unless changes are made. Please see later chapters on Social Security).

How Governments Fail

Why do governments engage in self-destructive policies that hurt long-term growth rates by depressing saving and investing?

It's because most of our politicians are myopic. They understand economics about as well as they understand Iraq or Afghanistan or their predecessors understood Vietnam. Those were places where the United States waged disastrous wars that cost our country in countless ways.

They believe the biggest factor in a thriving economy is consumption. Many times you will hear that consumption is 60 percent or 70 percent of the economy. Yet everyone can't consume. We also need some people to save—for their own good and for the good of the economy—and we shouldn't punish them. We should applaud them. It is the high savings rates of many Asian countries that raised their living standards, according to the great money manager John Templeton, who we will discuss later on.

Nevertheless, most of our pols both right and left urge people to spend and spend. They help people to live beyond their means by having the central bank, the Federal Reserve, keep interest rates low. This is a form of price fixing, a kind of Keynesian policy. Cheap money policies encourage millions to buy homes, cars and other things that they can't afford.

They discourage saving.

This is a dangerous practice as even one of our celebrated central bankers admitted during the horrific mortgage disasters of 2007-2008. That central banker was Alan Greenspan. In his recent book, he writes of how the Federal Reserve Board made sub-prime loans available to many people of modest incomes.

"I sensed that the loosening of mortgage credit terms for sub-prime borrowers increased financial risk, and that subsidized home ownership initiatives distort market outcomes. But I believed then, as now, that the benefits of broadened home ownership are worth the risk." See page 233 in Greenspan's "The Age of Turbulence".

The shocking part of this statement is that Greenspan "learned nothing and forgot nothing." That's even though his disastrous cheap money housing policies led to a recession and nearly caused a depression.

His policies were felt by tens of millions of Americans. They didn't follow the ideas shared here and lost their homes. Many were still hurting a decade later. Some may never recover. I can't do anything about reckless central banks (Mises in his book "The Theory of Money and Credit," warns government central banks are dangerous).

By the way, I call Greenspan "celebrated" because, for many years before the crash of 2008 he was lionized in the press as the greatest central banker who ever lived.

An example of this is the idiotic biography of Greenspan entitled "Maestro." It was a very bad book written by a journalist with no background or education in monetary issues, Bob Woodward. Even supply sider economist Lawrence Kudlow was caught up in the Greenspan mania before the crash of 2008. He called Greenspan a "great" economist in his 1997 book "American Abundance."

Yet the crash was in large part the result of a series of mistakes that Greenspan and his political buddies helped create. So even though millions of people of modest incomes couldn't afford a home, or a big one in a ritzy neighborhood, public policy in most democratic nations over the past few generations encouraged lenders to make credit terms easier and easier for buying homes and everything else. Go deeper in debt, is the implied message.

Buy! Buy! Buy!

That leads to more sales of everything. That makes people feel good for a while. But cheap money also leads to low savings rates as well as higher and higher rates of default. When a recession or even an economic slowdown happens, millions of people can't pay their bills. They have little or no savings. They have no cash emergency fund to get them through bad times. Having sufficient cash reserves is a critical issue for millions of Americans. It is an issue that we will discuss later. The point of this book is to change this mentality of spend a lot and don't worry about the consequences.

Yet what's wrong with consumption? What's wrong with wanting to have that new appliance? Or that trip to France? Or any of a number of countless other luxury items that can, in many cases, enrich our lives?

In principle, there is nothing wrong with these things. However, that's provided you're not a self-destructive consumer. But culture, lousy state education that requires zero money management courses, and anti-saving tax policies have created many mindless consumers over the past generations. That meant the wisdom of our grandparents was forgotten, or never learned.

The average American often spurns the values of our grandparents. Believe it or not, most of them saved and bought things with cash. So the culture of consumption, as with anything else, can get out of hand.

It can, has and will continue to destroy many lives. That's because it hurts the average person's chance to create wealth for himself and loved ones. That is unless he or she understands it and knows how to control it.

I give a personal example. Is alcohol bad? Yes, alcohol, like consumerism, can wreck a person's life if one doesn't know to control it; how to be the master of alcohol just as I propose to make you, the master of spending and investing.

My father, Alfred Bresiger, was a wonderful kindly man who, as befits his Austrian heritage, always had beer in the house. At the end of every work day, with his dinner, he would have his two beers and stop.

"Oh, I'm getting tired, Mary", he would tell my mother as he reached the end of his second beer. He never was drunk in all the wonderful 25 years I knew him, yet he packed away truckloads of beer. He controlled his alcohol consumption just as responsible people control their spending. They keep consumerism under control.

Consumerism can be smart. It can also be self- destructive. It can be the same as the drinking habits of drunks. For millions of Americans, it's the latter. It's up to you to decide how to spend the money that remains to you after sundry government entities have taken their shares of your hard-earned dinero.

This book is about making the right choices. One should never make any big spending choice before one understands the consequences. Here is the healthy approach to consumerism.

Smart Buying

Let's say you'd love to take that trip to Spain or you want to purchase a big, new appliance. After due consideration—not impulse buying—you get the best price. You're in no hurry to make a purchase. You ignore all high-pressure sales demands about buying now or missing the opportunity of a lifetime.

I often tell would be sellers at the outset that, in this first session, I won't buy their product; that I am taking their offers and will go to other places for comparison. Eventually you decide to make the purchase. You put it on a credit card. You select a card that has no annual fees, low interest rates and maximum rebate dollars. These are all features you can command. Why? You are the person who pays bills on time and has a top credit rating. My wife and I are at 805 because, for the last twenty-five years, we have always paid our bills off each month. We retired a 30-year mortgage about seven years early.

The bill comes for your trip or your appliance. You ignore the silly instruction about "the minimum payment." Within the 30-day grace period, you pay off the entire bill. That means you pay a zero percent interest rate.

You're a smart consumer.

You don't need a Carl Banks or a BrandX Loans shill or the phony promises of instant wealth from the mountebanks of the New York State Lottery. You dismiss all that as the same noise you hear when you pass Three Card Monte dealers on the street and keep on walking.

You're taking care of your affairs. You're on the road to the Financial Hall of Fame. It's a place populated by frugal people including legendary value investor Warren Buffett and Victorian philosopher of self-help Samuel Smiles.

Chapter 4

Budgeting, The Dull Subject That Can Save Your Life

"I don't know how much I'm paying for various things. I don't know how much interest I'm paying on my credit cards. I don't want to know what I'm paying for all these things. And Judas Priest! How did I run up this bill and in this ghastly amount?"

You can admit it.

Most of us have said these things some time in a life in which we spent money on so many things. Some purchases were useless. I said the above many times in my 20s and 30s. So this chapter is for everyone. It can help you live well below your means. That is one of the goals of a well-planned budget, a budget that also contains some money each month for savings and investment. The latter doesn't have to be a lot, but it must be done consistently over years.

Here, in a dull as dishwater subject called budgeting, is one of the secrets of how some people start with little or nothing, yet end up financially independent, knowing that they can meet every contingency.

Those who budget, those who know how much and why they're spending, have a much better chance of achieving wealth than those who don't. That's according to two authors who studied wealth creation. They say that those who build wealth all share at least one common characteristic that comes through budgeting: "They (the affluent) live well below their means". [The Millionaire Next Store. The Surprising Secrets of America's Wealth," Thomas J. Stanley, William D. Danko,]

They don't overpay. They don't engage in impulse buying. They don't allow screaming tube announcers to change their lives. They don't buy things because others are buying or because they just watched an infomercial.

Those who don't waste money are sensible people. They know what they're doing with their hard-earned bucks. This is critical in the race for financial independence.

Budgeting, how one spends, will help ensure your means of generating wealth won't be eaten up in overspending. It ensures that your income won't be wasted: You won't spend money the way the U.S government does. Our reckless government is recording record deficits and debts that will fall on the shoulders of future taxpayers.

It's 10 p.m.: Do You Know Where Your Money Is?

How you budget or, in some cases, whether you budget or not, can be the most critical factor in whether you can achieve your financial goals. Let's begin with the idea that, if you don't have a budget, if you just spend wily nilly, then you are like a person going to a place for the first time without a GPS or a map. You hope to arrive at the right place on time. Your chances are not good.

To achieve most goals in life you need a plan. It can be formal. It can be informal. It can be written. It can be oral. But there is an idea, an intelligent thought or set of thoughts, in how one spends money.

For example, my wife, the ever-comely Suzanne Hall, and I went to Las Vegas a few years ago. She wanted to gamble. I didn't. We agreed on a spending plan. We didn't make a big deal about it. But we knew what we were going to do and did it.

At the outset, we agreed on a set amount of dollars that could be spent on various things as well as on "gaming." The latter is the euphemism that casinos and those who push lotteries like to use to promote gambling.

I considered this money as an expense of this trip just as we would pay for food and lodging. We can spend right up to this amount and no more, I said as I gave her gambling dollars.

My wife had a set amount to play the slot machines. She lost it all. She enjoyed herself. She never asked for a cent more. What we agreed on is what we spent.

By contrast, I saw many people in the casinos who weren't following a budget. They weren't playing with an intelligent plan or any plan except, from time to time saying to a casino employee, "give me another stack of chips."

Unlike the people you see on the casino idiot box ads—where everyone seems to be winning, where everyone seems to be a jumping jack, where all the women seem to be super-models and are jumping into the arms of their delighted boyfriends—almost all those poor souls I saw seemed unhappy, tired, or both.

When you play a game involving quick computations, you're doing your opponent a great favor by playing when you're tired and more prone to mistakes, or when you're guzzling free booze as fast as they pour it.

Would You Like To Play Some More, Sir?

That's why the house never asks someone to leave the table when he or she is on a protracted losing streak and still seems to have some money left while big winning card counters are sometimes shown the door. That's also why the house gives you free booze, but forbids employees from drinking. By the way, the hotels will often give you cheap rates in Las Vegas. But that means getting to and from your rooms always leads you through their casinos. And they don't allow their employees to gamble.

The point is, unlike many of these poor souls in the casinos, we lived with a budget. By the end of the vacation, we were happy to leave Las Vegas with the bulk of our lifetime savings and investments intact.

That's more than one can say for many other poor souls vacationing in Vegas. When we received our bills for our vacation, there was no problem paying them the entire balance within the grace period. That's because they were just about the amount we expected. That meant the card company provided us with a short-term zero percent interest loan. We also earned rebate points that we later turned into cash, further reducing the costs of the trip. We also improved your credit rating---once somewhat below average at the outset, but today it is outstanding---because we paid the entire balance on time.

Motto of the story: Have a spending plan or budget for any substantial spending event or events. Don't think of it as a big deal. It can be constructed in any manner. If married, it is vital that both parties agree since they are jointly responsible for the household's income and spending. But the couple must recognize each other's needs and wants. They should also understand what's possible within their financial resources.

Patience is a vital quality in making a budget work, or almost anything else. One doesn't have to have everything all at once. One doesn't have to take four trips in a year; certainly not to Vegas unless one wants to engage in self-destruction. One or two can be enough this year. Then you'll have more to look forward to next year.

One also doesn't have to eat out three times a week. Eating out once or twice a week can be just as satisfying, a long-time financial adviser once told me.

"I had a client who was eating out several times a week. It was just too much. I persuaded him to cut it back to once a week," according to Lewis J. Altfest, CFP, a certified financial planner in New York City.

You Need a Budget

If you think you earn too much to have a budget or you just don't need any spending strategy, then you are making a mistake that many big earners and even big shot developers have made. [See the book "Trump: Surviving at the Top." Trump admits that, at one time when his real estate empire was in trouble, he had less of a net worth than a homeless man who had zero. Trump, through lavish over borrowing, admitted that at one time, in the midst of a real estate recession, his net worth was tens of millions of dollars in the red. Why didn't his bankers push him into bankruptcy? It might have taken years to unravel what assets belonged to Trump and which to the bankers. So they extended more credit and bet on Trump eventually turning around his fortunes, which he did.].

Even many people with big incomes often overspend and get into trouble. That's what the same financial adviser once told me. I came across the truth of his comment in a recent story. Altfest advises very successful professionals. These are people who tend to have annual incomes of between $600,000 and $3 million a year. The first time I interviewed Altfest years ago, on a story for "Financial Planning Magazine," he told me that he spent a large part of his time providing "credit counselling" for these big earners.

I was surprised.

"You're giving spending advice to rich people who are running up big bills that become unmanageable?" I asked in amazement. It was the amazement of someone who grew in the Southwest Bronx (the Highbridge neighborhood) and has never made and will never make anywhere near $600,000 a year. "Yes, certainly," he replied.

Living with a budget, or some kind of spending plan, is a vital part of a sensible financial philosophy. Without a budget—or call it a plan if you are bothered by the word budget—you'll end up reaching into your pocket again and again for your credit card to pay for various things. Often you'll spend with no idea of whether you're putting yourself into dangerous territory until the damage is done. Later, when the card company sends you the bill, you'll ask yourself: "How did I ever run up such a bill and how can I ever pay the entire bill at the end of the month"?

For millions of Americans, the answer is they can't, at least not in the short term.

Indeed, the long-term trend among American households has been to go deeper and deeper into hock. It is a trend we see in many other Western countries. Here in the states, over a 63-year period after World War II, the ratio of household debt to disposable personal income dramatically rose, according to Federal Reserve Board numbers.

"The ratio of debt to equity was $18.6 billion to 97.5 billion in 1945. By the third quarter of 2008 it had reversed big time, with $10.6 trillion of debt stacked up against only 8.5 trillion in equity," writes George Melloan in "The Great Money Binge, Spending Our Way to Socialism."

Some 16 percent of households had more debt than equity in their homes, he added. That means they were more likely to default.

That also means the average household's income was being overwhelmed by household debt. Those numbers have improved for many over the last decade but one should always be on guard for the dangers of excessive debt.

Will These People Ever Dig Out?

It will take many of these debt-plagued households' years to dig out. Many never will. The math is against them. Many ran up the debt through credit cards. They are trying to pay down their bills with something on the order of a 20 percent interest rate added to it.

Millions of American households are still trying to recover from the woes of the Coronavirus of 2020 or from the crash of 2008. Many have houses that are "underwater." The equity in their houses is less than the debt owed. So it is still very important to learn the lessons of troubled times or any times.

Those who budget, those who have a plan, who understand the extent of their bills and prepare to pay them off each month, don't have that burden. The difference between these two types of people is the difference between walking somewhere carrying bags of heavy groceries as opposed to walking somewhere carrying nothing or very little.

Who would you rather be?

The difference between the latter and the former is huge. It is the difference between happiness and misery. It is the difference between lying awake wondering how you'll ever pay your bills or having a good night's sleep, secure in the knowledge that your financial affairs are in order.

It is the difference between money madness and good financial sense. An important part of this approach is to understand the role of savings. Savings is a subject we will examine in our next chapter.

Chapter 5

Saving, Still Essential in a Sensible Strategy

"It is the savings of individuals which compose the wealth—in other words, the well-being—of every nation. On the other hand, it is the wastefulness of individuals which occasions the impoverishment of states. So that every thrifty person may be regarded as a public benefactor, and every thriftless person as a public enemy."

- Samuel Smiles from the book "Thrift."]

In a consumerist, "I want it right now" age, why save?

Given the policies of central banks across Europe and the United States over the last few years, savers seem to have no incentive to continue adding. So why should anyone save a cent?

A couple years ago I parked a $15,000 check in my J.P . Morgan/Chase bank's "high interest (sic) money market account." This was an example of an account that wasn't providing me with any reward for thrift. So what did I have in my account at the end of the month? I received an interest payment of less than a dollar. I didn't even receive enough in interest to buy a newspaper!

Our central bank, the Federal Reserve Board, until recently had a policy of dirt-cheap interest rates since the market meltdown of 2008 (Before the meltdown, the central bank also kept rates low, which some people thought was the cause of the meltdown). [See "Greenspan's Bubble" by

William Fleckenstein]. As a consequence of years of low interest rates/cheap money policies, they have had to raise rates. The fear is that, to prevent runaway inflation which is already far above the Fed's stated goal of two percent a year or less, the Fed must drive up interest rates so high that the nation will fall into a recession. Millions could lose their jobs and not be able to pay bills.

But the cheap money policy, endorsed with nary a peep by most major politicians, was advertised as a way of boosting the economy.

Easy Money

The cheap money has had mixed results. Indeed, when I began writing this book the growth rates, the GDP numbers, were declining because of the Coronavirus. But even before this disaster, they were weak here until 2017. That was same in most of Europe, where many economies were stagnating.

So given the Fed's policies always seem unfriendly to savers, why put money into a saving account? Why not spend every cent or put every dollar into investments that, in good times, would yield a healthy rate that can beat inflation and taxes?

It's because having a certain amount of cash on hand is something almost everyone should have in case you're laid off in a time of crisis or during a recession.

Previously we discussed the advantages of being able to pay your bills, especially your monthly credit card bills in full. I have said that avoiding the 20 percent interest credit card charges is a tremendous plus in the short term. It's great over any term. How many investments can guarantee a 20 percent return?

Remember, stocks long term tend to return about nine and half percent while bonds, depending on the kind, return about two to five percent. This advantage of avoiding credit card debt just gets bigger and bigger.

Indeed, say you maintain an average card balance of $5,000 a year over 20 years. That means you pay $1,000 a year in interest, not counting the $5,000 principal, and that comes to $20,000 in additional interest charges. Can you use an additional $1,000 in charges that you sidestepped each year by paying on time?

Paying your bills each month in their entirety is one of the characteristics of a financially savvy person. But there are other reasons to have adequate cash balances, cash balances that will carry you in an emergency situation, close at hand.

Can a Government Run Out of Money?

We live in difficult times. It is a time in which many nations are trying to recover from economic damage of long-term lockdowns. Governments are running up incredible amounts of new red ink. Even in the "good times" the government was running in the red. The same governments will likely be considering ways to raise taxes. Remember inflation is the ultimate stealth tax.

Again, I would like this book to focus on personal finances and how you can master them. However, it is necessary to remember what the government is doing and how it affects your goal of financial independence.

The General Accountability Office (GAO), in a report on federal spending, warns that "this situation—in which debt grows faster than GDP—means the current federal fiscal path is unsustainable." This government debt issue, which is hanging over all of us but especially younger Americans, is something I will discuss later.

The reason to have a substantial cash reserve at all times is, no matter how the economy is doing, bad times will come again so one should prepare. An old market adage is "the time to prepare for a bear market is in a bull market. The time to prepare for a bull market is in a bear market."

That wisdom should apply to your finances. You seem to be doing well now. Prepare for bad times in the stock market. They will come. I don't know when, but they will come. Governments can't outlaw the business cycle.

So your cash reserve should be designed to withstand almost any economic climate because, if you live long enough, you'll experience everything.

Do You Have a Reserve?

Even if you have a well-paying job, and both you and your employer are doing well—something fewer and fewer Americans can say today—prepare for at least the possibility of short-term unemployment at some point. This is something many workers, often through no fault of their own, will likely experience in their lives. There were times in my work life in which I was glad I had a part-time job to go with my primary job. In careers and investing, don't put all your eggs in one basket. Jobs are more and more uncertain. That's true even for the best workers.

So most advisers I have known say that one should always have at least three months of living expenses in cash. This is an emergency fund to get one through hard times.

The fund should be available in a bank savings account or a brokerage/mutual fund money market account with check writing privileges.

Given the unprecedented periods of long-term joblessness in the last recession some advisers say the emergency saving fund should cover six months. Today's economic woes are why. Many Americans had lost jobs, but have never been unemployed for such long periods. Some workers had to give up a job to search for another or even forever given the extent of welfare benefits some governments provide.

I know several workers who, in this economic crisis, had trouble obtaining unemployment benefits from the state in a timely manner. For instance, when the Coronavirus caused massive unemployment in New York, the state unemployment insurance hotline website crashed. It took many people weeks or in some cases months to get the unemployment insurance payments they were due.

So having at least three or as much as six months cash reserve to pay daily bills is commonsense. Knowing that, if the worst happens, a person has cash resources to pay bills. This ensures that you don't fall behind on credit card and other bills and incur penalties.

Here's another reason to always have some cash on hand: If you have built up investment assets, it is frustrating to start running them down to pay daily living expenses.

That means interrupting the compounding process, a big factor in building wealth. That means going backward in your attempts to achieve financial independence. Having an adequate amount of cash can be very important at various times.

Cash Is not Trash!

Indeed, there is another little-known reason to always have some cash. There have been short periods when cash, and cash equivalents, such as money market accounts, have been the best performing assets; better than stocks or bonds. Cash was gold, not garbage. More on this later.

So having cash on hand will likely be very important at some time, even though it often seems superfluous to many Americans, who see stocks and bonds as the better place to put money. Indeed, a recent published report detailed how about half of American households carry a credit card debt that exceeds their cash reserves. This is insane. They are playing with fire and should do their best to remedy the situation as soon as possible.

That recklessness will compromise one's ability to protect oneself in bad times or to take advantage of unique opportunities to improve one's quality of life.

For instance, my wife and I were married in 1987. At that time, we had just about nothing. I think we had about $1,000 in a savings account. Not much of a savings account; not much of a protection against hard times we were about to face. I still had a used car. Almost anything happening to that clunker could have eaten up our savings.

Still, we dreamed of having our own apartment, which would be the first piece of real estate either of us would own. Renting an apartment, which we had both done, meant getting no tax breaks and building no equity. By contrast, owning an apartment or house, under the American tax code, provides tax benefits and the ability to build equity as one retires the mortgage. We wanted to own for myriad financial and personal benefits.

In the first year and half of our marriage we rented and lived with a budget. We saved as much money as we could—about $15,000—and made sure we had no debt. When we tried to get a mortgage for our dream apartment in a better neighborhood, we started with considerable disadvantages: Neither of us had an above average income. We had no mortgage history. We were employed but neither was a star in our professions.

On the other hand, we also had one great advantage: We

had no debt. This was the result of sensible spending prac-tices—we didn't spend money we didn't have—combined with savings to ensure that bills were paid off every month even if one or both of us had a bad earnings period. The bank, after long consideration, gave us the mortgage. Not having debt saved us; it compensated for our lack of big incomes. Otherwise, we wouldn't have obtained the mortgage.

We barely made it because the bank was concerned about our low incomes and our ability to make mortgage payments. However, we obtained the mortgage, in part, because we had a good credit record. We paid off debts promptly and had no outstanding debt.

Finally, we owned some real estate. We owned a modest apartment in a nice neighborhood.

Don't Worry about the Depositors; Worry about the Bank

By the way, the bank, which later went broke, got a good deal. We never missed a mortgage payment. Through pre-pay-ments, we were able to retire our 30-year mortgage about seven years early. That's more than I can say about some of the financial institutions that handled our loan.

It's ironic banks worry about people having trouble with their mortgages. In our case, it was the reverse. We had two banks holding our mortgage, the Dime Savings Bank and Washing-ton Mutual, run into problems and were swallowed by other banks. Later we had a third bank holding our mortgage, J.P. Morgan Chase. Here the mortgage was retired. We owned a piece of real estate for the first time in our lives. Smart saving and borrowing practices were paying off. Later, we bought a second apartment with cash because we had been following sensible spending, saving and borrowing policies.

Sensible spending combined with saving ensured that we

achieved a goal that had eluded us for many years before our marriage: owning a home. Systematic savings over the first 18 months of our marriage was a critical factor since we just had enough for the down payment along with the costs of moving.

Saving for Independence

So why should you save? Why should you have healthy amounts of capital to shelter you and your family during hard times, times when prices advance at slow rates or, in extreme times, decline?

It is because the financial culture espoused here is one in which a man or woman doesn't want to be beholding to others. The person wants to pay his or her own way and never wonder what happens if a bank or a financial institution calls a loan or if an unexpected expense happens. The sensible person is ready for bad times. By contrast, there are countless stories of the millions of Americans who have nice lifestyles, who live in nice homes and drive cars, but they can't even raise a thousand dollars on short notice. This is dangerous. What if your car or some vital asset breaks down? What if a loved one needs help? Never let this cash poor situation happen to you. If it does, get out of it as soon as possible.

The smart investor can pay the emergency bill in cash or a credit card that he turns into a charge card. A charge card, unlike a credit card, requires that one pays off an entire balance each month by paying for the entire balance in the grace period.

This person then proceeds to re-build his or her saving. This kind of person believes in regular saving. That's even if he or she starts with a modest amount because this person understands that the mighty oak tree grows from the little seedling.

A Little Is a Lot Better than Nothing

Even small amounts saved over long period represent the first step on the road to independence. However, the person who consumes and consumes, with no thought of tomorrow, is on the road to poverty or a lower standard of living than if he or she had been patient. This person may seem to have a bright future, but tomorrow could be a disaster. That is as true as when a Victorian philosopher quoted at the head of this chapter recommended this idea over a century ago.

"Society at present suffers far more from waste of money than from want of money. "It is easier to make money than to know how to spend it. It is not what a man gets that constitutes his wealth, but his manner of spending and economizing", wrote the Victorian philosopher of self-help, Samuel Smiles.

"And when a man obtains by his labour more than enough for his personal and family wants, and can lay by a little store of savings besides, he unquestionably possesses the elements of social well- being. The savings may amount to little, but they may be sufficient to make him independent."

The next step to independence, after one has sensible bill payment practices and sufficient savings to back them up, is to start investing.

But investing isn't the same as saving. Unlike saving, investing means putting money at greater risk, giving oneself the chance to make, or lose, a good deal of money.

How does one go about this and start investing?

Chapter 6

Investments Part I

Taking Reasonable Chances to Achieve Wealth

To build wealth over the long term almost everyone needs to invest. But investing means putting money at risk, although the goal is maximum returns with minimum risks. That's an easy to say but difficult to achieve. One should only invest after one has taken the first steps in a financial plan: Have enough savings and a commitment to carrying no interest-bearing credit card debt.

We have discussed the importance of paying bills in their entirety and avoiding all monthly interest charges. Paying interest charges when they can be avoided is often the result of a lack of spending discipline or a toxic consumerism that will end any dream of financial independence. Paying monthly interest charges in most cases is the same as throwing away money.

Not all interest charges are bad. You pay interest on your mortgage. But then, there's at least two mitigating factors: You are paying down the mortgage and gaining more equity in your home with each payment. This is a kind of forced savings and investment because real estate values tend to rise over the long term. You are likely to sell someday at a higher price.

You reduce taxes by paying mortgage loan interest. When you pay interest on a credit card you neither get a tax break nor build equity. When you pay your rent, there's no tax break. Here is a part of a tax code that in which the renters are in effect subsidizing owners.

Are You a Sucker?

So paying interest charges to finance more consumer spending is the sucker's game in which you can only lose. It is a game in which you are giving away all the advantages to your opponents, the credit card issuers. They are delighted that you carry card balances from month to month.

Next, we looked at some of the benefits of sufficient saving. The primary benefit is it provides protection against hard times. I've seen plenty of those in the last few years. More may be on the way in the immediate future since the Fed is projecting a coming recession. Now let's go beyond saving to the next step in the plan of a financially sensible person.

Let us discuss investments. Why we need them and some examples of how to incorporate them into your plan. But remember investing is not saving. The latter has provided low rates of sometimes positive returns. Sometimes you have negative rates of return when one figures in the ultimate tax: inflation.

Why do I say sometimes?

In some recent years, savings interest rates were almost zero. I say sometimes because, when interest rates are low, your net returns, figuring in inflation, can be negative.

That is why we are also discussing investing. The goal of the latter is to beat inflation and taxes by a substantial amount. When you do that, you are improving your standard of living. Simple example: The long-term return of the stock market over the last 90 years of so is about nine and half percent a year.

That doesn't mean you get nine and half percent every year. It means if you consistently put money into good stocks or stock mutual funds, you tend to get an annual nine and a half percent long term-return. And we're speaking of 10 to 20 years or more.

The historic long-term rate of inflation has been about three percent a year in the United States, (although the recent number was far above three percent). Take out another two percent for taxes and the costs of brokerage—say about two percent—and you end up ahead with a "real rate of return—a real rate, a rate that figures in inflation—of about four percent (Nine percent minus three percent and minus two percent).

However, investing has no guarantees. You don't get nine percent or so every year. You can make lots of money on investments one year. Then, in the next year, you can lose huge amounts as we saw in the first part of 2020. But over the next four months, through the middle of 2020, the stock market wiped out its losses and was slightly ahead for the year by the end of July. By the end of the year, it was up by double digits. It was another good year for those investors who hung on through the bad times. Here's why it is ridiculous to try to time the market. We'll discuss market timing later.

Another example of the, at times, up and down world of investments is 2008 and 2009. In 2008, the stock market as a whole was down some 35 percent. I know many people who sold everything at the end of the year who told me they would never invest in the stock market again. Then these people outsmarted themselves.

It happened that 2009 was a great year for the stock market—it was up about 25 percent. For those investors who said they were done with stocks forever, they missed an incredible runup over the next decade. The S&P was up every year save one. Even in the down year it was only off by some three percent.

So remember: It's difficult to predict short term developments in the stock market. Therefore, it's best not to try. Follow a steady investing course over a long period; sometimes taking your lumps—but buying shares of otherwise good investments at discounted prices—and then getting rewarded later when markets recover. I will discuss this strategy later. It's called dollar cost averaging.

Steady as She Goes

Why follow a steady as she goes strategy instead of jumping in and out of the market, trying to pick a spot you believe will be a market high or low, a dicey strategy known as market timing?

It's because the same forces that increase the value of an investment, say a stock, bond or a real estate investment, can also just as quickly do the reverse. It's called volatility. That's what many stock market investors found out in early 2020, in 2008, 2001, 1973-74 and 1929.

Some readers are saying, why take the risk? Why not save some money every week, put it into a savings account and know that the balance will never decline?

Indeed, in a few circumstances, one can save one's way to financial independence. Unfortunately, they are limited to a very few people. And even the high earners have a disadvantage. They only earn high salaries for a short period. Many of them realize too late that these extraordinary salaries end sooner rather than later.

It's clear few of us can save our way to financial independence. Therefore, this book is for those with incomes in the middle. We must take some reasonable risks to achieve financial independence. Why must we take some risks and invest?

What Will Your Money Be Worth in 20 or 30 Years?

In a few words, your money will be worth a lot less unless it grows at a healthy long-term rate. The reasons are inflation and buying power. We invest because inflation will reduce our buying power over the long term.

"Even a moderate rate of inflation such as 3 percent will cut the value of a dollar almost in half in twenty years," says Liz Weston in "The 10 Commandments of Money."

That's because the system of central banks and big welfare states is expanding and almost never cutting back. That has a heavy price. It has meant persistent high taxes and inflation as governments run deficits, printing more and more money to pay for their often-reckless spending. This destructive process devalues a currency and a person's buying power unless the value of that person's assets beats inflation.

Indeed, as I write this, the government has taken on trillions of dollars of new debt to try to jump start the economy. The government doesn't have the dollars. So it will issue new money and sell more bonds, which is a form of debt that guarantees bondholders a fixed rate of return (That is provided the institution issuing the bond doesn't go broke). All of this reduces the value of our currency. You may have a lot of dollars in your pocket, but a devalued currency commands less in the goods and services you want as inflation devalues your standard of living. The bigger dollar balance is a delusion, tricking people into thinking they are richer. One has more dollars and feels rich. But somehow the money doesn't buy as many things as they did before the currency was devalued and inflation is reducing the standard of living. The buying power of the average person declines.

All this new money creation means one has to increase one's assets to keep up with inflation and ensure one's living standard doesn't decline. Governments print more money to pay the bigger and bigger bills as people live longer and expect more services from government. That devalues every dollar, pound or euro one holds. You have to increase your estimate of the amount of dollars you will need to be comfortable.

The inflation rate means the slow, or in some cases, the quick debasement of a currency. Whatever the debasement rate, some inflation—sometimes a little, sometimes a lot—is a constant of the modern welfare state. It's worse in the United States because we also have huge warfare state to support since America has acted as a kind of world policeman since the mid 1940s and has been expanding its welfare state at a feverish pace for decades. Both Republican and Democratic governments have been doing it. So these spending issues apply regardless of which party is in power and how much their election promises will cost a nation. I guess one way to evaluate these parties is one party is sometimes less bad than the other. But both, with a few exceptions, have been bad.

For example, in the United States, over the last century or so, the inflation rate has averaged about three percent a year. However, recently, at eight percent plus inflation rate, it seemed we've gone to the Disco Era. Back in the 1970s, there were years when the inflation rate was 10 percent. That was disastrous period for many sectors. I remember freelancing in the early 1980s for a weekly New Jersey publication called "The Sussex Spectator." I wasn't paid for the last four stories I wrote because the owner said he had to close the paper. He blamed it on high interest rates. Lots of other small businesses suffered the same fate as high inflation rates wrecked the economy as many smaller firms couldn't afford or couldn't get credit.

This was also a disaster for people living on fixed incomes.

Imagine you had retired and thought you have just enough for a comfortable retirement. Now all your numbers were no good because high inflation rates ripped into your buying power. Interest sensitive sectors of the economy, such as autos and housing, were also hurt the most as were elderly people whose prime earning years were gone.

Most purchases in the auto and housing sector are financed on borrowed money. Ten percent inflation caused the central bank, trying to stop inflation, to raise interest rates to 20 percent. That shut out millions of would-be buyers of various things because the price of purchasing those big-ticket items through credit was prohibitive.

There Goes Your Buying Power

So let's say you put your money in a savings account today. You earn less than one percent. Even as you accumulate more and more dollars, something bad is happening. It is something most politicians don't spend too much time dwelling on: The buying power of your currency, the ability of a set amount of money to command the goods and services you generally buy, almost always declines over time. That is unless your amount of invested money increases at a brisk pace; that is if it increases at a pace faster than the inflation rate.

I remember my mother in the last 20 years of her life. At the outset of her retirement, in her first five or ten years, her pension, Social Security and savings were enough but she had almost no investments that could grow faster than inflation. Later, as she had to pay much more for various things—such as prescription drugs, property taxes and everything else—her budget was much more challenging. Inflation had withered away much of her margin of protection. It became more difficult to enjoy the luxuries that she previously bought without a care. Some investments might have helped.

Therefore, one must earn a lot of a currency to make up for the power of inflation and that savings account won't do it. How do you accomplish this? You must find some kind of investing system that can beat the inflation rate over the long term, otherwise you risk seeing your standard of living decline. Avoiding that means successful investing.

So most of us want to beat inflation today. We also want to beat it for the rest of our lives, accumulating enough dollars or pounds or euros to ensure that, whether inflation is high or low, we'll be able to accumulate the kind of stash that will let one thumb his or her nose at the world.

If successful, one reaches a point in which one can rely on investment income and never have to make another cent again. What happens is you can live on the dividends and other income your investments generate, but never touch the principal. That is a wonderful goal, but how does one achieve it? Let's look at one way it can be done.

What's Your Lifestyle?

For instance, let's say today one wants to kick back—stop working—and thinks $120,000 a year income will create a comfortable lifestyle. Let's say one is not going to access a state retirement program such as Social Security for years, but needs income now.

Then let's say you have $2 million in investments and, through reasonable investments in the stock market, you are earning on average of six percent a year. Then you have achieved your goal. At six percent, without touching the $2 million principal and only using the amount of money your investments yield (capital gains, dividends, etc.), your investments provide $120,000 a year in income (I'm not counting Social Security income right now because, given its problems, who knows how much it will provide to the average tax-payer. For more on this subject, please see my later chapters on Social Security, including an interview with a key program official).

By the way, for some the risk of getting six percent in the market or in some other investment just isn't worth the worry. But one should understand the risks of investing, but also understand the risks of not investing, especially the person who isn't making or will never make $1 million or so a year and can never hope to save his or her way to financial independence.

So my plan is for the person with middle class income—say $50,000 to $125,000 a year—or even the person with less than a middle-class income but who wants to do better.

It is also for a person who has next to nothing or very little in assets and wants to accumulate what, for him or her, is a huge stash that will take care of the person for the rest of his or her life. Of course, much of this depends on what kind of life you want to live, where you want to live and how big a house you require.

Are you the person above?

He or she thinks $120,000 a year is a great income. Maybe you need more. Maybe you need less in annual income. But let's say the principal amount you want will be somewhere between $500,000 and $3 million. How does one get to somewhere between those numbers when starting out with nothing or less than nothing? Investing is a hard reality for these people. It is a reality that they must face.

Dear Mr. and Mrs. Middle Class or Would-Be Middle-Class Person: Given the proclivity of governments to take more and more of your income, and given the potential over the next few years of governments to cut social programs many people are depending on, it is unlikely, well-nigh impossible, that you can save your way to financial independence. You will need to take some reasonable risks. You will need to do some investing, especially in stocks. Long-term stock investing, carried out with a disciplined plan, is one of the few ways to beat the currency debasement.

So you, the average person who yearns for financial freedom, must put some capital at risk—must invest on a regular basis over long periods. In the next chapter, we will work with the idea that you are ready to invest.

Chapter 7

Investments Part 2

Achieving Financial Independence by Beating Taxes, Inflation and Avaricious Mutual Fund Companies

We're ready to invest for the long term in order to beat those pesky things that sap one's standard of living—taxes and inflation. Inflation is caused by too much money printed by the central bank chasing too few goods. So let us begin with a few sensible investment principles.

Investing Is a Marathon not a Sixty Yard Dash

You expect to make big money and achieve financial independence overnight? You're in the wrong place. Play the lottery and good luck to you. That's because you'll need it.

Get Rich Slowly

The majority of formerly middle class or poor people who either achieved wealth or became financially independent did it gradually.

How?

They consistently invested over long periods. They looked at investing the way they looked at paying monthly bills.

Investing is a regular expense along with other regular payments such as rent and food. They didn't skip months putting money into funds, stocks or bonds. They did it every pay period. These patient folks weren't discouraged because they lived through some bear markets. They didn't sell everything in 2008 or the early part of 2020 because markets sagged.

Here's a portrait of a smart investor who isn't panicky and invests month after month: From the time markets were depressed in March 2020 owing to the Covid crisis until a year later, the market, as measured by the S&P 500, was up some 53 percent! That's despite lots of his friends and neighbors who panicked and sold everything in the spring of 2020 or in 2008 or in 1987 or one of many other times when markets were depressed and seemed as though they would never recover.

Usually, the smart investor started with very little, but he or she stayed with it for 20 or 30 years.

These wise, patient folks are not flustered. They continue to buy good stocks even in bad times such as in the middle of the Coronavirus outbreak or in the middle of the first decade of this century. This constant buying strategy was explained by Wall Street Journal columnist Jason Zweig in an October 2016 "Intelligent Investor" column. He said that by sticking to a plan of buying stocks in good times and bad, these smart investors enjoyed not one, but several bull markets.

For example, the S&P 500 Index lost money over the first decade of this century (-1.2% a year from 2000-2009. That led many commentators to call it the lost decade).

But for patient investors, those who were investing in the market some 35 years, from 1976 to the end of 2011, the returns were good. The S&P index gained 10.6% a year. A person who was investing each month, month after month in bad as well as good times, did very well. However, some investors never got anywhere near that. They jumped in and out over those 35 years. These without investing discipline never received anywhere near 10.6%.

Why?

They didn't stick to the program. That cost them dearly. Many lost their biggest chance to obtain financial independence. The point is to stay invested over long periods. Don't try to guess when markets have made new highs or lows. However, many play the fool's guessing game.

Dalbar, an investment research company, has done studies documenting how the average individual investor often self-destructs. The company has shown how a particular fund gained 11 percent in a year, but the average investor in the same fund only gained about half as much.

How could that happen?

The investor jumped in and out of the fund over the year. He often missed the best days of the market. He thought he could choose the best days and avoid the worst. He was wrong.

That's why many average investors never seem to obtain good long-term returns. They have no plan. They do tend to have huge costs. Why? Every time you get in or out of the market, you generate costs. Warren Buffett doesn't agree. He often buys stocks to hold for decades or for a lifetime.

So what's wrong with trying to call market tops and bottom. This poor record of many individual investors is because the market tends to go up and down in short spurts. It is well-nigh impossible to call these spurts beforehand, jumping in and out of the market. It is better to invest consistently over long periods. It is also sensible to do the reverse when you retire. You should disinvest slowly in retirement. (For more on the latter, please see my later chapter at the end of the book for retirees or those near retirement).

Be Rational and Avoid Emotion

The coach with the most national championships in American men's college basketball history, UCLA's John Wooden, said that one shouldn't get carried away by victories or depressed by defeats. Don't get too high or too low. Anyone who is investing over the long period will experience highs and lows. Live with them.

Bad investors reacted irrationally at the bottom of a market. For example, I know of several people who got out of the market in the horrible year of 2008 and swore they would never invest in the market again.

Guess what happened?

The next year, 2009, was a great year for the market. And a year like 2008 can be good over the long run for patient investors. That's because in a bear market year they get to buy some stocks at bargain prices. That's when no one seems to want them. They go on sale. Later, the patient long-term investor is rewarded for bargain hunting patience. A solid, sensible approach offers you the wisdom of history and says use it.

Get Started Early

It doesn't matter that, say, you're only putting $100 a month into stocks or stock funds as long as you are consistent. You can always increase the amounts later on as you make more money. What matters is to start as early. Don't put it off. It is also important that you stay with it—you don't break into your investments for frivolous purchases and ruin the compounding process—and that you start early. The more years you buy stocks or stock funds, the better, the less dangerous investments are, and the more bull markets you will likely enjoy.

Longer Is Better

Think you're at the end of your journey? Trying going a few more miles. It can be a big payoff. Just a few extra years of investing can make a huge difference. Here's an example: Say you commit to putting $500 a month into stock funds for 30 years. Say they earn a yearly average of nine percent—not a great return, but not a bad one. After 30 years, you have $1,481,924 before taxes. Terrific.

But let's say you continue the program for just five more years. You continue to put in $500 a month and again you earn nine percent a year. O.K., you have more. But how much? A lot more.

You have about $900,000 more, or a total of $2,358,215. Those five years increased your final total by about 60 percent! Victory goes to the patient; to the person who realizes how important the compounding process is and gets the most out of it.

Longer is better, even if it is just by a little. If you can hang in with an investment program even for an extra year or two or get started as early as possible, do it. The compounding effect, if you put it in place and let it go on as long as possible, can make almost anyone financially independent. Albert Einstein is credited with saying that compounding is "the eighth wonder of the world."

Compounding is a huge factor in creating wealth.

Watch the Expenses

One of the characteristics of a smart investor is that he or she doesn't waste resources. In other words, he or she is a cheap (fill in name). In my case it is my nickname in Spanish. (*El Mas Tacano de Todos*. Translation: The Stingiest of Them All. My wife, the ever-comely Suzanne Hall, says if I were president, the United States would have no deficits or debts. However, we'd all be walking around with holes in our shoes). But there is a lesson here: How often does one throw away money on ridiculous things. Then a good opportunity comes along to invest or purchase something useful at a big discount. You must pass on it. You spent your money on the superfluous.

Don't throw away money on credit card interest charges. Those are resources that can be used to make you rich. This common-sense idea is no different for investment expenses.

In anything that you try, always consider the costs of accomplishing it. Costs matter a lot in investing. This is a piece of wisdom that was countlessly said by one of the best friends the individual investor ever had—John Bogle, the founder of the Vanguard Funds.

Vanguard was once a pipsqueak of a fund company when it was founded in the 1970s. Vanguard was ridiculed for using the new investing tool of low-cost index investing. Today it's one of the great fund companies.

Its incredible success is not just because it, like many other fund companies, has gathered a lot of assets and the company is profitable, with many of the company's big shots rich. It is because it has made millions of average people much better off. It has allowed many of us to achieve financial independence and say good riddance to the egregious E-train. Thanks, Mr. Bogle.

Let's talk some more about mutual funds. The average domestic stock fund, according to the fund rating service Morningstar, has an expense ratio of about 1.3 percent or 1.4 percent for a managed fund. The latter is a fund that is managed and runs up big brokerage expenses because it does lots of trading and is often changing the portfolio.

Why does it spend so much of your money?

It's because the fund managers often can't make up their minds about which "hot" stocks they want. They often buy as well as sell a lot. The problem is that you pay for their indecision because every time someone buys or sells stocks the manager is triggering a bill. (And when they buy lots of shares, it often drives up the price of the stock, which makes it more expensive for the company to buy, or what trading pros call market impact costs. All of this drives up costs and, of course, you are handed the bill).

By contrast, let's look at the average expense ratio of a good index fund. It is a passively managed investment. That's because it does little trading. Its passive management means its expense ratio on average is only about 0.2 percent. It invests in its stock index—possibly the S&P 500 or the Nasdaq index—once a year and it is done trading for the year.

That's about 1.2 percent less you're spending on your managed investment each year. Remember, the lowest costs are the goal of investors. That lower cost promotes better performance. The superiority of using low-cost funds, funds often called passive or index funds.

In the short term, the larger expense is no big deal. But over the long term, ten, twenty or thirty years, it is huge; you're paying through the nose. This "I'm not wasting my money" philosophy can amount to tens of thousands of dollars in savings for the average investor. It is critical in long-term investing success.

That's money that stays in your pocket. That's money that doesn't go to the mutual fund company or their favorite brokers. That's money that doesn't buy yachts for your advisers and snazzy offices for the fund company. Many fund companies spend money like they were running the federal government. Whether under left-wing or right-wing administrations, they seem to spend like it's going out of style.

I don't like to see any of my fund companies advertising during the Superbowl.

Why?

That's the most expensive ad space over the course of the television year. Who pays for those ads? You do.

I figure the ad money is coming out of expenses that are passed on to me as an investor. By the way, I've never seen a Vanguard or TIAA/CREF commercial during a Super Bowl broadcast.

Be a Finicky Consumer

Ever notice how when some people get control of your money they can start spending it like drunken sailors? Many fund companies—like lawmakers raising taxes to finance more programs they think will keep them in office or allow them to run for a higher one—aren't thinking of how they spend your money. You have to look out for your money. It's your property. It doesn't belong to the mutual fund company.

That means that whenever you use a financial product—such as buying funds or a stock—you approach it the same way you go shopping: Compare costs. Then ask questions.

For example, say you hire an adviser to put together a financial plan or you hire a broker to buy securities for you. (Later, I'll have some recommendations on advisors).

How do these advisors get paid and how much? You want to know what they are getting paid in comparison to other financial professionals. The price of investments can be one of the important issues in buying a security, as we have seen. It can make a huge difference in your returns and whether or not you achieve your goals.

Consider a sports team as an analogy. To win, it is important to score a lot. But it is also important, perhaps more important, to prevent runs/points scored against you. Winning in sports, or investing, means limiting scores against you or investment costs that reduce your returns.

By the way, I am a New York Yankee fan. I grew up four blocks north and west of Yankee Stadium. In the concluding game seven of the 1960 World Series, the Yankees scored nine runs. That's usually more than enough runs to win an average game. But for my Yankees that day, they gave away a lot of runs. They got sloppy—the same way a lot of funds are run—and the Pittsburgh Pirates scored ten runs and won the game and the World Series. Limiting costs and mistakes, in investments and baseball, matter. Over the long run, costs matter whether we are talking about a particular investment or a financial professional you use.

How Does He or She Charge and Conduct Business?

Compare prices. Compare how they conduct business because some are fiduciaries—a legal requirement that a professional must put the needs of the client before those of himself or herself—and some are not and will be taking care of their employer before they take care of you. I will also discuss this later.

Fruit Shopping on Metropolitan Avenue

Let me give an example of this shopping around, looking for bargains, principle. Most days I used to buy various fruits when I lived in New York. Blueberries were my favorite. But just because they're my favorite is no reason to overpay. When I lived in New York, two blocks away from my apartment house, there was a fruit stand. Across the street was a small supermarket with a big fruit section. I never bought blueberries without surveying the prices at both. Quite often they were different. All it took was a walk across the street—watch the traffic as you cross Metropolitan Avenue; many drivers still think they're driving on a nearby highway—to determine if there was a bargain available.

Rarely were the prices the same. Sometimes I bought blueberries for a dollar or two dollars less a box just because I checked; just because I dodged the cars. Do the same with investments. Check before you buy investment products or services. Shop around. It can make a big difference.

Never throw away your money. There are plenty of pols who are happy to do that for you every day unless, on the rare occasion, someone stops them. That doesn't happen in the advanced welfare state. The latter is a state in which almost every major party assumes that more government is always better and that will get them elected or re-elected. The truth is the opposite. Less government is better government, but don't tell that to our career pols.

We have discussed why we invest and some of the broad philosophies of investing. Before we go on to some more investment specifics, I believe there are some readers who are saying: "Yes, it makes sense to invest over the long term, but I haven't got any money to do that now. I'm not sure I ever will."

That's a fair criticism. But is it true? Often, I believe it is not. Almost all of us, at one time or other, have been wasteful.

Now to this skeptical reader I ask: Before turning around and dismissing the premise of this book—that the intelligent management of money can make most people financially independent and that many people with middle-class incomes can succeed—please read one more chapter.

For the rest, those who are ready to invest and want specifics, I ask for patience. It won't be a waste of time.

Indeed, in the next chapter I will have some advice on how you can find more money to invest more than you thought.

But first, let's pose a question, a question that I have posed to myself and to others many times: How does the average person—people like yours truly and many of my friends and neighbors, a kind of person often referred to as a "working stiff"—someone who doesn't make fabulous money, someone who is not a partner in a bigtime law firm or CPA firm or a quarterback on some great football team—find money to invest?

Not letting investment money get away, money that could be used to build wealth, will be next. Let's find some money. Let's use it, or most of it, to build an investment program that makes a person financially independent.

"Tempus fugit," (time flies)

"Wealth is what you accumulate, not what you spend." ["The Millionaire Next Store," Thomas Stanley and William Danko. p1]

But thrift is not a natural instinct. It is an acquired principle of conduct. It involves self-denial—the denial of present enjoyment for future, good—the subordination of animal appetite to reason, forethought, and prudence. It works for to-day, but also provides for to-morrow. It invests the capital it has saved, and makes provision for the future. From Samuel Smiles' book "Thrift"

Chapter 8

Getting Started, Using Thrift to Find Investment Money That's All Around

"I can't find the money to save."

I often hear this from people who often have decent incomes. Change that mindset with a step.

Just take the first step on the financial independence road.

Otherwise, the opportunity to invest will be lost before you know it as time flies by.

Don't worry that you are starting your investment program with small amounts so maybe it might be better to wait until you have more. Don't tell yourself that you'll get started next year or five years from now or after you get married or when you see your United States senator riding with you on a rush hour F-train.

Don't think that you'll get started when your favorite relative dies and leaves you a bundle. Don't tarry or it will cost you a chance at financial independence.

Do it now. Do make a few sacrifices today for a better tomorrow. Do start with small amounts, if that's all you have.

Doing a little is much better than doing nothing. That's because "it is better to light a candle than curse the darkness", according to Peter Benenson, founder of Amnesty International.

Why is there no time like the present?

Saving and investing over long periods are the ways that most people get rich. The longer the period, the better. The higher the rate of return, the better. But it is time—how long you follow this program, how long your money compounds—is the most important factor in achieving financial independence for you and your family.

Let's begin with a very small amount. Can you find a paltry $1.66 a day to put aside? That's right. One dollar and sixty-six cents. Maybe you put aside your spare change every day.

Sometimes I see spare change on the street. Few people seem willing to bend over and pick it up. I do. It's a good bending exercise.

The spare change strategy, over the course of a month, comes to some $50. What can a lousy $50 a month amount do?

A lot over decades thanks to compounding.

Just Start with $50 a Month

If you put $50 a month into a mutual fund—every month—and never increased the amount. And say you earned an average of nine percent a year over 40 years, what would you have before taxes? You would have some $235,822. That's pretty good for just putting your spare change aside and investing it.

Now $50 a month is less than $2 a day. That is not beyond the means of many Americans, some of whom each day pay $6 or more for a cup of java that they can make at home for a fraction of that. And $100 a month may not be too much either when one examines how much money people often throw away though reckless spending practices. Of course, with $100 a month, you'd have double as much—$471,644 after forty years. Again, that's a nice piece of change.

For many in their 50s or 60s, with some other savings and their pensions/Social Security, if they just had an extra few hundred thousand dollars so many things would be possible and life could be so much easier. I think of Judy, the elderly woman who I mentioned. A few hundred thousand dollars would make a huge difference in her life.

But again, I can hear the doubters: "Sure, the loose change money concept might work and I might come up with $50 a month, but I would never be able to find $100 or $200 a month to invest. That's just too much."

Really?

We'll now look at some common, wasteful money practices that almost all of us—like me before I earned the much revered "Tacano" title; a title I was given because I stopped wasting money—have engaged in at one time or another and may still be doing today. Let's look at some ways that one can raise a little extra money that can be devoted to investments.

Do you take a train and a bus every day? In New York City, the basic subway fare was raised a few years ago to $2.90. Since the wasteful government state agency running the trains and buses is losing hundreds of millions of dollars, there is talk that it will have to be raised soon Massive red ink and bad service seem to be the trademark of all advanced welfare state enterprises. That's because almost every business "enterprise" the government runs ends up in the red.

Assume you use four fares a day. You ride a bus to the subway. Ever thought of walking to the subway? Ever thought of saving five or six fares a week? Let's say you save $14 or so a week because you hoofed it more. There's a little more than your fifty dollars a month. There's your sleeker body. There's your first step down a lovely road called financial good sense. There's a signpost up ahead that says financial independence.

Rancid Apple Cabs

If you use cabs or Ubers in New York City or in almost any congested big city—you often pay part of your considerable fare just to sit in the car. The cabs often get stuck in traffic with the meter going and going—and if you can find a way to reduce or eliminate your use of them, then the savings are huge. Yes, many people can save $50 or even $100 a month just by walking a little more. There are other ways to generate more geld through smart spending.

I search for the best credit card rebate deals. When I don't get them, I look for a new card and there's always some-body ready to offer me a better deal because my wife and I have excellent credit. We didn't always have a good credit rating. For example, when we were married, we had little in savings and assets as well as sometimes carrying credit card balances from month, our rating was low, in the 500-600s. Today it is in the 800s.

So now we get the best deals. I would estimate that today I am getting about $50 or more a month back in rebates. Why shouldn't the card companies give it to you too? You're giving them your business and you pay on time because you believe in sound financial principles.

When you shop do you go to a supermarket chain that pro-vides you with a chip card that guarantees you will always get the store discount on an item and records your savings through the year? I do. So far this year I am on course to save some $400.

Besides that, I often use coupons that can save me another $200 or more a year. Grand total of my shopping strategy: $600 a year in savings. Again, there's your $50 a month.

Need an extra $50 or $100 a month? Do you like dogs? Many people have started dog walking businesses or just pick up a buck sometimes walking our four-legged friends. In New York, you can sometimes earn about $6 per half hour doing it. Do three hours of work a week and you have $36 or more. In a good month, you'll have $200 to invest.

This idea works well with almost any part-time job. That's because two hundred dollars a month invested over 40 years and earning nine percent annually makes you almost a millionaire. It gives you $943,286.

It doesn't have to be dog walking. Many people have various skills that they could turn into a home business. I'm thinking of talented people in my neighborhood, or almost any place, who have foreign language and music skills that could be turned into extra income.

This extra income could be used to fund a saving and investing program. But, while looking for more income, also remember to play defense: Look at ways you can cut out or reduce needless spending.

Do you eat out a lot?

I know some people with good incomes who eat at top restaurants three or four times a week and some of them tell me they have difficulty finding money to invest. I'm not surprised. Why not, I tell these people, eat out two times a week—cut back at least once a week. Projected savings of two people dining out one less time a week in New York at a good eatery: About $100 a week or more or some $400 a month that can be devoted to investing.

However, let's only use $300 of that a month and only do it for 30 years, earning nine percent a year. What happens? You have $553,342 before taxes. Add another ten years to that investing program. You have almost $900,000 extra or close to 200 percent more—$1,414, 929.

Some of these smart people could end up owning a restaurant! It's all because they spent and invested wisely. They had sense.

But let's look at the big stuff.

I go into my local bodega and a guy ahead of me hands over a $20 bill. He asks for his favorite brand of butts. He ends up with his smokes and the clerk returns just $8 bucks. Twelve dollars a pack!!! I'm shocked every time I see it.

Were you thinking of giving up smoking? Well, there's your investment money. Twelve bucks a day comes to $360 a month. Combine that economy with a small part-time job that yields $140 a month and you now have two things: Much better health and $500 a month in additional income. What does $500 a month over 40 years, earning nine percent a year give you? You end up with $2,358,215.

Santa Maria, you're going to be rich and live much longer!

But, as they say on those irritating overnight tube infomercials, "But wait. We're still not done."

The Bad Dream

My *bête noire* of overspending is the cost of owning a car in a big, expensive, city like New York, the land of high taxes and pols with itchy fingers.

Years ago, when I lived in a rural area, made a modest income and needed a car for my job, I noticed something: The persistent, endless costs of keeping the car on the road prevented me from accumulating a significant amount of saving or investment. When I came back to New York City and lived there for some 30 years, I tried holding on to the car for a couple of years and regretted it.

In New York City there is an extensive mass transit system. Granted, the mass transit is a shabby, often dangerous, state system. It is run by a non-accountable public authority, the MTA. The latter has its headquarters in the most expensive part of town and passes on its incredible bills to the overburdened taxpayers. Its lousy, often ancient, trains frequently shake.

Still, the decision to use mass transit and avoid the costs of running a car might be the most important move a middle-class person makes in building or not building wealth. When my wife and I came to our apartment in New York City in 1989, we sold our car so we could afford the purchase of our first apartment. I would estimate that, over decades of living there without a car, we have saved on the order of $300,000.

That's a lot of money.

That doesn't even tell you the true value of what we did. If we tried to bring home an additional $300,000 in cash, we would have needed to earn $450,000 before taxes. That's a hell of a lot of E-train rides going to and from work. In New York City that means going to Manhattan.

So that $300,000, or $450,000, has made a big difference in our lives. That's because a lot of it went into savings and investments. Some of it went into luxuries we enjoyed and paid for with real, not plastic, money. That meant more big savings in not paying credit card interest charges.

I acknowledge that some people can't follow this tip; that many must have a car as I did when I lived in small towns in the 1970s and 1980s. The best reason to own a car is because you live in an area that has little or no mass transit. The next reason for car ownership is for business. You must have one to earn a living. Then you can deduct some of the costs from your taxes. But, if you don't need a car, just consider the savings and the investment opportunity of not owning one or having one instead of two.

They are huge.

In New York City, the city and state governments have declared war on the motorist. They levy incredible taxes, fees, fines, tolls and God knows what other costs. (Congestion pricing; charging motorists to drive into the center of the city is the next outrageous scheme to mulct taxpayers).

It isn't much different in most other big cities. What if one could find a way to do without a car, or maybe live with one instead of two or three cars? The opportunities for investing would increase. I estimate it can take $10,000 to $12,000 a year to run a car in New York. That includes car payments, maintenance, insurance, repairs, fines, towing etc. Some people here pay $1,000 a month for a car.

Is it worth it? Each person must decide, but I believe it depends on your work and where you live. But examine the alternatives.

Turn Your Car into Millions of Dollars

Take a thousand dollars a month you spend on a car and instead put it into a mutual fund that earns nine percent a year. What do you have before taxes in 30 years? You have $1,340,933. O.K., once again we'll play our do it for another ten years game. Then, you have $3,428,845!

Do you think an extra $3.4 million will make a difference over the course of your life? Most Americans won't make three and a half million dollars over a lifetime.

Again, I emphasize that not every person can or should do this. But if you can, do it. My point is I have known lots of people who didn't need a car for business or who lived in areas where there was mass transit, but they insisted on owning a car for the status or convenience of the car. I was one of the latter. I'm glad I left the car owners club. So is my waistline.

I believe the savings from ditching my car has made a big difference in my life. I doubt with all the full-time and part-time jobs I have had, or will have—I continue to work part-time because I like to work at certain things; things that I now choose to do, not things I must do—that I will end up making $3.4 million.

Thank God that in the middle of my life I learned how to play much more effective money defense. I avoided many needless costs.

By the way, today my wife, Suzanne Hall who also walks a lot, and I, starting with nothing at the end of 1987, have more than enough money to buy a car with cash. We could avoid the financing charges that drive up the costs of so many cars.

And you know what? I don't want one. I prefer walking and I do so a lot; about six to nine miles a day. I do a lot of shopping on foot. I am 71 and my former long-time doctor, who has hundreds of pages on my medical history, once said that I "have an athlete's heart." There aren't a lot of seniors who can and do walk six to nine miles a day in part because they don't have a car.

I think the source of many Americans' health and financial problems is too many car rides. It is a lifetime once expressed to me in the question of a friend who was told that she had to walk a block to a meeting place.

"Isn't there parking nearer than that," she asked. By the way, this kindly woman, a friend of my wife's, suffers from numerous health problems.

Yet from time to time, I rent a car for a few days. Then I hand the 2,000-pound monster back to the rental company and it becomes its headache, not mine."

The thrift techniques that I have outlined here aren't easy. But what is the alternative? Spending almost all or all of your income can mean a life of worrying about finances. It is one of having to rely on others who may or may not be helpful in your time of financial need. These people who rely on others are hurting themselves, as Samuel Smiles, the Victorian philosopher of self-improvement, warned. [Once again, see "Thrift," along forgotten book of timeless wisdom. You can find it online].

It's About More Than You

Indeed, the thrift techniques I advocate while, at times a bit difficult, are by no means impossible for most people with middle-class incomes. Indeed, you can even become so used to them that, after a while, you take them for granted if you're investing on an automatic basis. They call for a bit of discipline and the will to improve one's self.

Remember, achieving wealth doesn't have to be all about you. It can also mean that, because you have managed your finances so well, you are now able to help others. You can give more to charity. That's because you have accumulated considerable assets. My wife and I give much more to charity today in part because we can.

But before one can do things for others, the sensible person will improve his or her standard of living, ultimately achieving financial independence.

To do that, says the poet Robert Burns, means "To catch Dame Fortune's golden smile. Assiduous wait upon her. And gather gear by ev'ry wile. That justify's by Honour. Not for to hide in a hedge. Not for a train attendant. But for the glorious privilege of being Independent."

Now, we're ready for the next step on our road to independence. We have now established that most people have some potential sources of income and savings that they didn't know were around. And these are only a few of the ones I found. If the average person looks at his or her own life, I believe more can be found. You're now ready to commit to putting money into investments.

What kind of investments should one use?

Chapter 9

Investing Techniques for the Long Term Investor---Patience Required

The long-term returns of the stock market, with all its ups and downs, have almost always beaten inflation and taxes over 10, 15 and 20 years. However, within those long periods there have been shorter periods when the stock market was a horror show. One such period was the beginning of March of 2020 owing to the Coronavirus. Through the first few months of the year the market was down by 20 percent. Then, just as many were dumping stocks, the stock market made an incredible recovery. For 2020, it was up for the year about 15 percent. So what started out as a bearish year turned into a bullish one. The people who got out when things looked bleak, who locked in their losses, must have felt like fools.

They should have remembered that there is always the possibility that some unexpected event can waylay your plans to achieve financial independence. This means that the sensible investor must be a person who is patient. This person is in the market for the long term---20 years to 40 years. He or she agrees with an ancient philosopher who said that "he who has patience can have anything."

So this kind of person believes that the surest, safest way to financial independence is achieved slowly. One becomes rich by each week or month putting money into good investments—ones with low costs and proven long-term records such as Vanguard S&P 500 Index Trust, among others—on a regular basis and having the right mix of investments.

The right mix is called asset allocation. For instance, say you only invested in long-term government bonds over 85 years between 1926 and 2011, your rate of return was 5.7 percent a year. However, say you had a portfolio that was half stocks and bonds over the same period. Your rate of return was almost 50 percent better at 8.3 percent. That was a huge difference. The numbers are from Ibbotson Associates.

This right mix means stocks, bonds, some cash and a little bit of alternative investments such as gold or real estate. (Alternative investments, such as gold and other metals, are the ones that tend to perform very differently than the stock market. Their performance has little or no correlation with the stock market. A little of them in a portfolio can be good. But be careful. Never invest in anything you don't under-stand. Always make your investments as part of a long-term investment strategy).

What's the Formula?

The asset allocation formula can vary from person to person and can also vary based on a person's age as well as goals. One follows this formula for years. Investing, as many people learned in the market meltdown of 2008, can be dangerous in the short term. That's a lesson we were re-learning from 2020. That is why one is much more likely to do well by staying the course for long periods than by trying to make "an overnight killing" or by jumping in and jumping out of the market. This is based on the spurious idea that you can always pick market lows or highs.

But that also means that one must approach investing with realistic expectations. The stock market, based on historic returns, doesn't provide 20 percent returns every year. In-deed, based on its long-term history, one year out of three, it tends to go down. However, its long-term return is about nine percent and change a year. That might not sound fabulous. And, in the short term, it isn't.

Still, getting a little more than nine percent a year, say over 20 years, could be remarkable. It could build a fortune for almost anyone willing to sock away a few hundred dollars a month over a few decades. Say you put $500 a month, or $6,000 a year, into an investment that earns nine percent a year over twenty years. You've invested $120,000 over the period. What do you have, not deducting for taxes? You have $336,448.

If you started ten years earlier and invested $180,000, you would have a bit more. You would have $922,237! Get going!

So the sensible investor doesn't expect to make millions of dollars over night. He or she is a long-term investor. That make a fortune overnight person, you may know, is a sucker. The "I might make a million" overnight investor is playing lotteries.

Is it impossible for this person to get rich?

No, it's not impossible. But it is unlikely. The chances are so stacked against him or her that this person is unlikely to ever achieve financial independence. Remember, although one person does win the grand lottery prize, governments that run these Three Card Monte schemes never talk about the millions who play these games and never win a substantial prize.

The Sensible Investor

The person following sound financial principles, with a long-term plan of consistent investing in good stocks, bonds and mutual funds, backed by sensible spending polices, is much more likely to accumulate a huge stash. This ensures that the investor's buying power—the ability to command goods and services that maintain his or her lifestyle over multiple decades—is protected. That means the value of his or her money outpaces taxes and inflation.

How important is that?

Very important.

Say you have $50,000 a year in income and that is just enough for you to live. What do you need to maintain the standard of living years from now? Let's assume that the traditional inflation rate of the past half century or so in the United States continues in the future. What will you need in twenty years to match today's $50,000? You'll need an income of $90,000 a year just to stay in place. You'll need to increase your yearly income substantially. Successful investing is one way to do it.

That is why we are going through how to invest on a regular basis. Investing is something that has both risks and rewards. This chapter and succeeding ones examine strategies for maximizing the latter and reducing the former. The greater the risks one takes in investing, the greater the potential rewards or losses. It is important to understand both.

The sensible approach to investing calls for taking risks while reducing potential losses. It may be described as enjoying a few drinks at dinner, but not getting drunk.

It is a balanced view. It is the idea of having dessert, but not every night. Dessert every night means ending up in the same state as the majority of Americans—fat or obese, exposing oneself to myriad health risks such as diabetes.

When you invest you should remember at the outset—it's not all desserts and bull markets that go on forever. There's going to be lean years. You need to know how to survive them.

But, if you stick to a consistent discipline, a discipline of investing in good times and bad, and if you have the proper mix of different kinds of investments and if you don't get carried away by unrealistic expectations—and yes, there are a lot of ifs in this sentence, which appears as though it will never end—then the chances of obtaining a strong return and attaining goals are good.

Don't Make Mistakes

First, let's state the Warren Buffett rules of investing: Rule number one: "Don't lose money." Rule number two. Don't forget rule number one." Just as we have stated elsewhere on other money topics, so too this is just as important to investing: Mistakes will kill you.

What mistakes?

Getting carried away in a bull market and putting all your money in stocks or all of it in just one stock (Remember some former employees of Enron who kept huge amounts of their assets in their company stock. That became worthless because of the hijinks of Enron official Kenneth Lay. He was the man President George W. Bush called "Kenny Boy.").

Getting depressed in a bear market, believing it will never end and refusing to buy good stocks that have become bargains in the midst of bad markets. For instance, in the spring of 2020, in the midst of a market crash, a long-time successful money manager said times are tough but this is a good time to continue a regular buying plan because some good stocks, given time, will come back.

Besides not having a consistent buying plan that will make money for you over the long term, there is another mistake many people make: Not buying more than one kind of asset, not having a diversified portfolio. The latter means having some bonds as well as stocks.

Bonds in some five-year periods have beaten stocks. For instance, the first years of this century were so bad for the stocks—but not so bad for bonds—that it was called "the lost decade". That's because, figuring in inflation, stocks made nothing in the first decade of this century. Yet, in the last five years of the 20th century, stocks, as measured by major indexes, were earning 20 percent a year each year, far outdistancing bonds. I don't know if we'll ever see five consecutive twenty percent yearly returns again. I doubt it, but I'm not smart enough to know for certain.

When will bonds beat stocks again?

Yes, sometime they will but I don't know when. People who tell you they know the exact direction of stocks and bonds over the next year or two are often charlatans. They are just trying to separate you from your hard-earned money by claiming they have found the Holy Grail of investing.

The key is you should have both stocks and bonds for the long term. What percentage of which depends on your outlook. Are you a moderate, aggressive or conservative investor? How many years do you have to invest?

For example, I am a "young" senior citizen. I am investing with the idea that I still have some 20 years to go. Today, I am some 50 percent stocks, 40 percent bonds and 10 percent cash. Some might say that's too much in stocks for a man of my age. But lifespan keeps increasing. I have good health. So I believe that, even though my wife and I are in good financial shape, we could still use some growth, even at our age because maybe one of us, or both of us, may make into the 90s or even beyond. That means we will need more money to live comfortably than we thought twenty or thirty years ago.

Stay the Course

For those starting out, I believe in a consistent buying pattern over years or a consistent selling pattern if you are retired (For more this, please see my chapter on strategies in drawing down retirement assets). So a large part of sound investing is the same thing that makes champions in any contest: Understand that everyone, no matter how smart, makes mistakes.

Even the great Buffett came to regret his investment in U.S. Air. Buffett later sold his shares in the airline. To his credit, he questioned the investment and wondered how he could have made such a mistake, especially in putting money into an industry in which costs, plane fuel, were difficult to predict.

His public acknowledgement of a mistake is one reason why I have respected Buffett. He has a great record, but he is a modest man who admits and even broadcasts his mistakes, infrequent as they are.

However, minimizing mistakes is how to succeed. Avoiding mistakes comes from being careful and profiting from past errors. It also comes from observing those mistakes of others. This acknowledgement of your limitations promotes a humility that recognizes and profits from errors.

Still, if you invest long term, you will make some mistakes. You should expect it, says money manager Kenneth L. Fisher. The goal should be identifying errors you're likely to make and try to avoid those. Failing to stick with an appropriate strategy is a major error many investors make.

One way to avoid or minimize mistakes is through the use of time. By committing to a realistic long-term investment program—a sensible program that mixes different kinds of investments—that can weather bad times and good, one increases the chances of doing well. Let's discuss how and where to get started. Let's discuss a dollar cost averaging.

Chapter 10

How to Go from a Little to a Lot and Take the First Steps to Financial Independence

Let's start building up assets. Let's start going down the road leading to financial independence.

The person who achieves a goal, has at least two important characteristics: this person has patience and a balanced investment approach. This means he or she is ready to commit to spending discipline and to investing on a regular basis, such as each pay period or once a month, over the long term. That also means he or she will use different kinds of investments.

This is an approach that reduces risk. This sage investor doesn't put all his or her investments in one stock or even just in stocks or does all his or her investing over a short period. Indeed, what happens if the investor dumps a bucketload of money into the market when it is about the make new highs and is now oversold?

No, the smart investor has a diversified plan for today, tomorrow and ten years from now. He or she also has a mix of stocks and bonds as well as a few other things. He may own his or her house or apartment in an expensive city, expecting to sell it at a profit and later move to a cheaper city. He or she may own a second apartment or home as an investment.

Many argue the asset allocation decision is the most important factor in investment returns. Asset allocation means how you distribute investments. What percentage goes to stocks, bonds, cash and real estate etc. The most common long-term asset allocation, for those with twenty years or more to invest, tends to be sixty percent stocks and forty percent bonds.

Ken Fisher, a long-time investment adviser and money manager, makes that argument. He writes that correction asset allocation is critical to any long-term investment plan. Having diverse investments in a plan is very important, he believes.

One can't get from Point A, someone with little or no assets, to Point Z, someone with substantial assets, enough to achieve financial independence, without a road map.

Why, an adviser such as Fisher asks, are you investing without a long-term plan? The sensible investor puts his money in more than one kind of investments. These are called asset classes. These investments include stocks, bonds, real estate and other things such as cash, such as money market accounts.

Buy on the Cheap

Some of the principles the smart investor uses include: Buy low expense investments, preferably index funds, and be sure you mix your investments. The latter should include both stocks and bonds, but it should never be just stocks or just bonds. You should also have a bit of cash, which, in bad times, can be your best investment. The reason for diversification is that no one can know with certainty if the next investment cycle will be bad for stocks or for bonds or any investment. Bonds and stocks tend to move in different directions. Stocks, long term, perform better than bonds.

So why not put all your money in stocks?

If you are an aggressive investor and if you are very young, with decades to recover from losses, an argument can be made for a stock only approach for a while. But most people don't have limitless time to invest—I only started in my late 30s—and many people don't have the stomach to hang in for decades to get good returns. They often interrupt their efforts to spend on what often turn out to be superfluous things or they stop investing because they are facing a bad period. In some periods, not all or most, bonds have beaten stocks. When? I'm not sure. But I know, that over almost any given 20-year period, that it will happen sometime.

So the most important thing the investor should remember is don't put all your eggs in one asset class basket. This way, when stocks are down, your bond investments will likely be doing well. In a diversified portfolio, the reverse will also happen—a bad time for bonds will mean stocks are doing well.

Diversification carries the investor through rocky times. It doesn't guarantee that he or she will never lose money. But what it does is give one a better chance to lose less in bad times. Example: Markets were down in the United States in 2008 some 35 percent to 40 percent. I know some people who lost 50 percent and they vowed to never invest again.

Did my wife and I, who had bonds as well as stock funds, take a hit?

You bet. But we were "only" down some 25 percent because we were diversified and had not put all our investments in one thing, or asset category. We had a fair amount in bond funds. Our losses in 2008 were painful, but not as painful as for many other investors.

So we survived into 2009. That's when markets recovered. We got some of our losses back from the previous year. Indeed, the stock market over a decade until the recent crisis of early 2020 was a great place, but it doesn't always do well.

Recently more bad times have come for the stock market, but I don't know when they will end and neither do most people. It will depend on some factors that are unpredictable. Example: Who could have predicted a couple of years ago that the Coronavirus would have such a profound effect on the economy and markets?

So, since the stock market tends to go down one out of three years, and since the stock market has been in a long-term bull market, the odds are good that, sooner rather than later, we'll get a bear market. Indeed, now, owing to the Coronavirus, we were in one, but it turned out to be a short bear market, only lasting a few months.

Still, diversification, which helps limit losses in rocky times, works for the patient investor who is a long-term player, especially younger or middle-aged investors, with a long investing time line. Indeed, for the young investor, with 30 years or so in front of him or her, a bear market at the outset would be good. You would be buying a lot of shares at discounted prices that would later be big winners whenever the bull market came roaring back.

Where's Your Investing Roadmap?

A long-term plan is a sensible, reasonable approach. The plan doesn't have to be anything huge. It can be a one-page or less plan. It doesn't even have to be a written plan. It can be a mental commitment to saving and investing in a certain way that you can state in a few sentences. It can and should be reviewed at least once a year. But you should have some kind of a plan. It doesn't matter that you're starting with nothing or little more than nothing. What's important is to start as early as possible and to have the discipline to survive and invest through bad times and good.

The great investor Sir John Templeton began with nothing, but he and his wife made a commitment to save and invest large amounts of their income no matter what. For more on this see the book "Investing The Templeton Way" by Lauren C. Templeton and Scott Phillips. Templeton and his wife, at one time early in their marriage, committed to investing 50 percent of their income. But there is no need to be that radical. In most cases, committing to ten percent at the beginning of a plan would be a good start. Then as you begin to make more and can afford it, adjust the investment percentage upwards.

Some sixty years after beginning their investment plan, the Templetons were billionaires. So make a commitment and a plan. Be sure to include other family members who would be significant players in achieving wealth. Husbands and wives—pulling in the opposite directions—often ruin any chance for financial independence.

When my wife and I were married we had almost no assets, which is the same perilous position of tens of millions of Americans today. We had a used car. It was on its last legs and it was draining our cash. We didn't need it and got rid of it. The latter is a case of how playing defense helps you play better offense. With no more car insurance and other maintenance costs, we had more money for everything, including getting serious about our investments.

Thank God that our marriage was strong enough that we could agree and execute a financial independence strategy. This agreement was critical. We both spend money in a sensible manner. We both have to save or invest to achieve anything. We both have to make the money. We both have to agree on a money strategy. We both would prosper or fail together. We both won.

Our plan was to get rid of our car. I was delighted to get $100 for the sale of the clunker. We put the money we weren't spending on the car into investments every month, which was a big payoff. We also signed up for our retirement plans at work. Our employers were willing to match our contributions to a certain extent. We tried to save enough cash for a down payment on an apartment in a nice neighborhood.

It was seminal event in both of our lives. We would own the apartment. It was the first time we owned and not rented our housing. That meant our apartment represented another kind of saving. It was an asset that we could sell our apartment someday or borrow against it. It was also an asset that the government would subsidize through tax breaks. We had never received these breaks on our housing prior to that because we rented.

The nicer neighborhood had better shopping, less crime. We would be able to live without a car. That would be a huge saving; freeing up money for savings, investments and also fun things such as taking trips, which sometimes included renting a car.

When we started our new plan, we were renting an apartment, owned next to nothing and lived paycheck to paycheck, even though we were both employed. The previous sentence describes how millions of people live through most or even all of their lives.

Why did we and millions of Americans live like this?

In the United States the cultural emphasis is on consumption. That means very little of the average person's income, no matter how healthy, finds its way into investments that will make them independent. People are, in effect, making a bad bet. They are betting that they will always make great or at least decent money and won't ever happen to worry about putting money aside for a rainy day or for a time when they won't have big paying jobs. Yet that's something that happens to most of us.

For example, I worked for the Sunday New York Post Business section for some 19 years. Then, owing to Covid, I was fired along with others in March 2020. I was sorry but my wife and I had plenty of money to survive. My editor apologized and said I would be the first hired back when things turned around. He was a nice guy. Three months later, he was gone.

People who don't allow for these potential life changing events such as the above are taking big risks. To you, the person struggling for a better financial life so he or she can provide for others, I say: I want you to have what we have. My wife and I now have financial independence as well as control over how much we work or don't work.

I quit my full-time job a number of years ago when I was 57. I did it for a number of reasons but the most important was this: I could afford to do it.

I have never been tempted to take on full-time work since the happy day I left a small publishing company that was coming apart and where my respected boss had been fired. My new boss wanted me to stay. I would have nothing of it. I had enough of the seedy subways and office politics. I gave three weeks' notice and left my full-time job. However, I did agree to do some freelance work from home for the company, which was later sold and later welched on my freelance contract. Thank God it wasn't 20 or 25 years before. Then it would have been a difficult to leave a job I had started to dislike but now it didn't matter. My wife and I had plenty of.

What a great feeling! My wife later quit her full-time mechanic job at Delta Airlines, which she had enjoyed but came to hate after a decade.

How did we get to financial independence?

Early in our marriage, we made the commitment to saving

enough to put a down payment on an apartment and putting money into a good mutual fund at an initial rate of $100 a month. Later, as we both earned more, as we entered the prime earning years of our work lives, we invested more and more.

We agreed to invest a set amount of funds every month in good times and bad. This is a strategy that is called dollar-cost averaging. This consistent buying strategy reduces investment risk over the long term. When the fund's share price is going down, you are getting more shares at a bargain price. When share prices rise, your balance is rising. You are rewarded in good times for your patience during bad times. Again, it is a strategy that tends to work very well over long periods of 20 years or more.

We used a low-cost balanced fund at the outset, the Vanguard Star Fund. That's because it is an all-purpose fund that gave us a mix of both stocks and bonds. It is a good idea for those who can't afford to buy both a stock and a bond fund. This balanced fund was a diverse investment that would never shoot the lights out in bull markets but would avoid self-destruction in bad markets because it wasn't as risky as the all-stock approach.

Over more than 25 years of holding and adding to the fund, it has provided what we wanted, about nine to ten percent a year long-term. We still have some money in that fund because it is a sensible, conservative fund. Here is a true "Tacano" fund. It is a fund that has some of the lowest costs in the investment industry, an industry that sometimes abuses the small investor as I will detail later.

As we earned more and as I took on extra work, we put more into our investments. We raised it to $200 a month and, over about a decade as we both earned more because we were in our prime earning years, we increased it to as much as $1,500 a month spread over five funds. This was besides contributing to our retirement plans at work. It was a lot but no, we never starved ourselves or stopped taking occasional vacations.

These investments included stock, bond and cash funds. They also included paying off variable rate mortgage early. We had several different kinds of mutual funds. We also had some stocks and bonds. Besides our retirement plans at work, we each opened individual retirement accounts (IRAs). We saved for retirement through these qualified—qualified as in special, reduced tax, treatment—accounts for several reasons: One, in our early years of marriage, when we had low incomes, they gave us immediate tax breaks by reducing our current tax liability. That's always a big issue when you live in a taxing place like New York. Two, as these accounts built up, we paid no taxes on investment gains, which would not be taxable until between the ages of 59.5 and 70.

Tip: Wait until age 70 or whatever is the latest age if you don't need these retirement funds. (By the way, as this book was being put together, there was a move in Congress to extend to required qualified asset disbursement age to 73 or 74. If you can, take advantage of any extensions and let your retirement money compound as long as you can. Then, if you can, take the minimum distributions from your qualified retirement accounts). The longer tax-deferred compounding takes place, the better. Remember how we have shown that even just a few extra years of compounding can make a huge difference. As per the advice of numerous financial professionals I have interviewed over the years, don't expect Social Security to be a big part of your retirement income.

I will discuss these issues as well as the woes of Social Security with an official of the program in later chapters. He concedes that changes must be made in the program. Don't wait for them happen because the changes—if they are like previous changes—won't be good. Yet changes are inevitable because the system is running in the red. Prepare now.

Keep adding to your qualified retirement accounts in your 60s if you are still a part-time worker as I am. If you have a Roth IRA, you can continue to contribute forever as long as you have earned income, up to $7,000. (That number might be upped). It could be increased owing to inflation. You never have to take assets out of a Roth IRA and when they come out there are no taxes. That's because, unlike a traditional IRA, you never received tax deductions.

Still, although this book is about how to start with little or nothing and accumulate enough to make you financially independent, I also have a chapter for those who have already accumulated a nice amount and are close to or in retirement. It's important to understand how to protect these assets in retirement, which were built up over decades.

One caveat of using these qualified retirement fund assets: My wife and I have a lot in our retirement accounts as do millions of Americans. As I write this, there are various pols who are coming up with schemes that would grab some of these retirement assets, changing the rules that often make these accounts a good deal for millions of Americans.

Be on guard for money grabs. That's because the government is becoming hard up for cash. When people or institutions are hard up for money—whether they are advanced welfare states with aging populations or crack addicts desperate for the next fix—they will do outrageous things they normally would never would do. Desperate governments—the same as desperate drug addicts—could hurt all of us who saved over decades.

How did we do?

We had triumphs—fat markets in the 1990s when we sometimes made 20 percent or more a year—and we had some disasters, the first decade of this century when some people told us we were idiots for investing. Overall, we made a little more than nine percent a year over the long term. That is what I set out to do; earn the long-term market return. I wasn't trying to get high returns—say 20 percent a year—because the risks one would take to achieve it would sometimes mean you end up losing 20 percent. I haven't tried to hit homeruns every time at bat because home run hitters often strike out. I'm happy to hit a lot of singles and not strike out much.

However, it was still a rocky ride, one in which we were sometimes tempted to turn back. We realized a truth at the outset: the sensible investor doesn't expect to become rich overnight. That's for those poor souls who plan on winning big in Vegas, or at any of the thousands of casinos that are sprouting up everywhere like venereal diseases that can't be contained.

These casinos are supported by many pols as a form of economic development. That idea would be comical if it wasn't tragic. Remember, the casino scam is a place where the house has every advantage and no one advertises your odds against winning big.

Avoid the get rich mentality of the casino. A long-term investment plan means patience. The patient investor is putting money into good investments on a systematic basis—every month, every pay period or every week. The patient investor is ready to do this for 10, 20 or perhaps 30 years. That depends on how much he or she needs to achieve financial independence.

Still, the sensible investor is the tortoise, not the hare. The smart investor is happy to make steady progress. This person understands that it is better to light a candle than curse the darkness. That's because the latter screams and hollers, but accomplishes nothing. The former starts one toward the achievement of a long-term goal, even if it is only the first steps.

So focus on regularly putting money into good investments. We'll see later these include low-cost index funds. It doesn't matter that you start with small amounts. What matters is that you start as soon—tomorrow or, better yet, today or yesterday if you have a time machine handy—and that one sticks to a long-term strategy.

That means put money into funds in good times and bad times. That's when one can buy shares of some excellent stocks or bonds at bargain prices. These are shares that will likely later become profitable when markets recover.

Besides that, sign up with the mutual fund company—a good one that has low expense funds that do well, but never shoot the lights out. Vanguard is one. There are other fund companies that can help. Don't look for a fund that has just had the best performing fund numbers. Next year it will often be a dog.

Look for a fund or fund family that consistently does well over a five year or a ten-year period. Fabulous returns frequently are the result of luck or a fund manager taking a big chance one year and hitting a home-run (For more on this, please see the chapter on how this year's big winners often become next year's bow wows). Often those factors will reverse the next year and the fund will go from best to worst.

Want an example?

Look up the history of the roller-coaster American Heritage fund run by manager Heiko Thieme. I once met him at a conference decades ago. Thieme was an example of how dangerous the fund industry can be. He was an electrifying speaker, but I'm glad I looked beyond his considerable charisma in investing my own money.

Indeed, the fund hooked lots of investors who did poorly because they bought the fund just after it had a fabulous year. His fund was volatile. He would have a great year every once in a while—maybe earn close to 100 percent. Then he would advertise these numbers to the hilt and bring in lots of new investors. They thought they were also going to get 100 percent. Then the next three years the fund was egregious. Investors wondered what happened. He was the free agent in sports who sells himself just after he has a fabulous year and everyone starts bidding on him. He gets a long-term contract. He never hits those peaks again.

In investing and in other situations in which you are making an evaluation, it is important to remember: Sometimes a manager does well because he or she is talented and executes a certain kind of investing style. But sometimes a manager's perfect storm is unlikely to ever happen again.

However, other times a person who has a big year was just lucky. The manager is unlikely to ever turn in outstanding numbers ever again. Some fund companies don't care about the latter scenario. Like most pols, they just care about getting your money. They want to accrue as much in assets as they can. That's how they, and often not you, make a lot of money.

For example, I can remember the complaint of John Bogle of Vanguard, one of the greatest money managers and investment thinkers. In a kind of "where are the customers yachts" comment, he said that many investment companies do very well for the people who own them. However, the people who buy the shares in their mutual funds they sell to the public don't do as well.

In following a systematic investing plan, don't count on yourself to take the money out of a checking account each month or pay period and put it into investments. Have the money automatically deducted and put into the funds. If you have to mail in money each month, it's amazing how funds can often end up spent on other things.

The Patient Investor

Why do I emphasize a long-term view of investing, the idea of getting rich slowly?

First, expecting to get rich quickly, through some lucky break, is dangerous. It doesn't happen. Indeed, the opposite does.

Second, another reason to be patient is one doesn't appreciate fast wealth and what it represents. It is very easy to lose that kind of wealth; it's similar to what happens to many average people who win the lottery and then end up broke.

How many times have you read about sports stars and one-time superstar entertainers who made a lot of money in a short period—such as sports stars who received huge signing bonuses—and, a few years later, had gone through all their money and were broke? It happens.

Why?

Sometimes they had no tax reduction strategy and much of their income in their prime earning years was eaten up by Uncle Whiskers and his merry band of publicans. The quick overnight wealth made these athletes/entertainment figures reckless with their money. They had no system for maintaining wealth.

By the way, ever notice that a lot of sports stars live in Florida even though they weren't born there? It's because, once they come into the big bucks, their financial advisers/lawyers tell them to move there. State taxes are low there compared to states like New York and New Jersey.

Over the course of a long-term contract, Florida residency can save huge amounts of money. That's money they may someday need when they aren't making big bucks.

Coming into huge pools of money in a short period can

trigger a tax problem. All of a sudden, in most advanced western welfare democracies, one can be paying a high tax rate if one suddenly receives a lot of money. Warning: If you are going to come into a huge pool of money, don't accept it until you have consulted with a CPA and or a qualified tax adviser—also a certified financial planner—before you start spending it.

Human nature can also be the friend or the enemy of your wealth. Your money will get eaten up much faster than if you slowly accumulated assets. But what if you make it and lose it fast? It is unlikely that, in a lifetime, one will repeat the big earning patterns. You get one chance at your prime earning years.

So one must remember to get the most out of these prime earning years. They are unlikely to happen again. But one key is this: put aside a healthy percentage of your earnings year by year. Ten percent is a good beginning.

How do you accumulate significant assets, the slow patient way, when you're not a big earner?

You make a commitment to saving and investing, despite all the pressures to consume that come from all quarters every day. These are pressures that come from mass media. Here are some examples of them that come bursting out at you when you turn on the tube: "But you must act now. Call now! Operators are standing by. If you don't buy now, you will die tomorrow so act now."

The last was an exaggeration, but not by much.

If you're an average earner, there is that wretched thing that exists in every country. It will likely be your biggest expense. So be warned: Governments' misguided spending and taxing policies often destroy would be wealth. Here's an irony: In the long run governments are hurting themselves. That's because, with less wealth generated, there is less to tax!

If the government wanted to generate a lot in tax revenue, it would keep tax rates as low as possible, giving people an incentive to work harder because they would get to take home more of their hard-earned geld. That may seem counterintuitive. But nevertheless, it is true as I detail at the end of the book.

Indeed, supply side economist Arthur Laffer sums up this philosophy when he says, "We want more, not fewer, billionaires." To which I would add: We want more Americans to be millionaires or at least to be well off. More and more people getting wealthy is good; good for the economy, good for individuals, good for governments that are always hungry for more money. It is good for everyone. The more my neighbors get rich, the more likely I am to do the same. The more, the better, because high net worth individuals are often paying a lot in taxes compared to the rest of us. A few years ago New York Governor Andrew Cuomo was begging the rich not to leave the already high tax Empire State. When they leave a state or city in big numbers, those staying there will have to pay more in taxes. The poor, the middle class are hurt. When big numbers of the well heeled come to a city or state, its economy tends to prosper.

Still, governments tax savings and investments. In Western countries, in the advanced democratic-welfare states, they treat savings and investments as though they were plagues instead of the building blocks of every healthy, growing society that the world has ever known. This was an idea explained in the great economic tome "Human Action." The latter is a classic work by Ludwig von Mises. Mises used to write that all of us who benefit from a prosperous economy are standing on the shoulders of our parents and grandparents who saved and invested.

How do you benefit from their wisdom?

Small Amounts Can Become Big Amounts

It doesn't take a lot to get started on the road to financial independence. It should be as much a mental as well as monetary commitment. Tell yourself that, no matter what, you will make a commitment to save and invest starting now.

Try to designate ten percent of your income as a starting point. If you don't make a lot of money—say you make $30,000 a year so you are saving/investing $3,000 a year—it doesn't matter that you start modestly. It matters that you start with something as soon as possible.

Is $3,000 a year, or $250 a month that much? For most people, like young and middle-aged employed people with lots of prime earning years ahead of them, I don't think so. And I say it as someone who used to make less than $30,000 a year for a lot of years.

That's because one of the biggest reasons why some people achieve financial independence and others don't is a factor that has nothing to do with being rich or poor or smart or not or even which investments you choose. It is something that equally affects the humble and the well-heeled—over long periods

Over time the compounding effect, the ability of money to create money, becomes more and more powerful. The sooner one starts money compounding, the more years one has, the more likely one is to end up with large assets. That's the sentiment of one of the smartest money people I have ever come across.

"One of the most important concepts to accumulate wealth and becoming financially independent is understanding the time value of money", writes Staten Island, New York CPA John J. Vento. "By far the most valuable asset we have is time, but unfortunately it is usually something we take for granted and then do not fully appreciate until later in life."

[That's from Vento's excellent book "Financial Independence: Getting to Point X."]

Fine, you say, I'm ready to invest on a regular basis. What are the best kinds of long-term investments? More in the next chapter.

"To catch a thief, appoint a thief."

This is a comment attributed to President Franklin Delano Roosevelt when he appointed Joseph Kennedy as the first head of the new Securities and Exchange Commission (SEC)

"There are two things people should never see being made----laws and sausages,"

German Chancellor Count Otto von Bismarck

Chapter 11

Where to Invest and How

Many in the financial services industry—big brokerages, big fund companies, high-priced advisers—want you to invest their way. That means using pricey products that are good for them, but often lousy for the average investor. The piggy ones—brokers with sales quotas, the fund companies with high-cost structures including lavish advertising budgets that get included in their outrageous fund expense ratios—hope you will never see them making their financial sausages. They're often rancid and overpriced.

Yet many in the business want you to buy high priced products. They are often manufactured by their employers and cost the client much more than the easily obtainable plain vanilla competitors.

Why?

They often get paid more in commissions when you buy their employers' products, even if they are lousy, overpriced and inappropriate for the average investor. One of the goals of a smart investor is to identify those bad products that eat up precious investment dollars and avoid them. Substitute simple easy-to-use investments that achieve long term financial goals at the lowest possible costs.

The plain vanilla funds are better. They are the simplest, often not-advertised, products. They tend to be better performers over the long term, but many investors don't know this.

Investors often focus on what happened in the last quarter or year. They want quick, overnight wealth. They are excited by some sales oriented financial professionals who believe their company's funds or investments are fabulous. The sales jockeys—men and women with sales quotas—will make promises that are unachievable. At the height of a bull market, many investors develop unrealistic expectations.

I remember, at the end of the 1990s, when markets were returning 20 percent a year, there were people who thought they were being ripped off because they didn't get more than that. They opted for riskier and riskier investments. They turned their backs on the plain vanilla options that offered them the best chance to get good long-term returns.

So this chapter explains why low-cost index funds are the best choice for most beginning investors.

And they are also better for many people who have already accumulated some assets. By the way, Warren Buffett has said that, for most individual investors not willing to do through investment research to find the best stocks, index funds are usually best.

Different People Reach the Same Conclusion

In going through the reasons why low-cost index funds are the best investment for most individual investors, I will rely on experts such as John Bogle, the founder of the Vanguard Group of Funds, and Wayne H. Wagner, a stock trading expert who has been an adviser to money managers and studied how costs affect investors.

I will also cite one of the analysts who was caught up in a huge Wall Street financial scandal—Henry Blodget. For many, he was the ultimate financial industry sleazebag. He was an example of how the financial services business, like most of big government, puts its interests before those of the individual.

Blodget is a former Merrill Lynch analyst who was thrown out of the securities business. He had been recommending stocks his employer was pushing that he knew were losers for the investors but great for his employer. Why am I including the once sleazy Blodget as one of our guides to obtaining good returns and building up a nest egg over the long term?

Like Bismarck and Joe Kennedy, Blodget knows how the tricks are played. That's because he played many of them.

So Blodget, in a mea culpa book, "The Wall Street Self-Defense Manual. A Consumer's Guide to Intelligent Investing," tells you why index funds are your best investment. You don't have to like Blodget to like the book, which is candid and clear. In admitting his sins, Blodget explains how and why to avoid some of the worst investments.

It reminds you of Bismarck warning you about sausages and bad laws. It is the same reasoning that led FDR to appoint Joe Kennedy as the first head of the United States Securities and Exchange Commission (SEC). That's because Kennedy, who pulled a few shady deals in his time, knew all about bucket shops. Indeed, the idea of finding the right person to root out a rogue is that "it takes one to know one." It is the idea that it takes a thief, or a reformed one, to catch a thief.

A bucket shop was a sleazy, unregulated brokerage where the average investor was often cheated. Blodget, like Bismarck and Joe Kennedy, knew all the tricks of the game. He knew them because he pulled many of them and he also knows how to steer clear of them.

Blodget's recommendation to avoid getting rooked?

Use index funds.

For most, according to investors and managers as varied as Warren Buffett and Peter Lynch, index funds are the best way to amass wealth for someone who is committed to a long-term investment plan. An index fund is a passively managed investment. Instead of buying and selling securities in an actively managed fund, index funds fill out a portfolio, such as the stocks of the S&P 500, just one time a year.

Which wins? Active or managed funds?

Four Out of Five Mangers Lose

In most years, only 20 percent of actively managed funds will outperform index funds. Some are saying, let's find and invest with those active fund managers. However, here's the problem. Those 20 percent star performers one year will not be the star performers in the next year as we noted in the case of Heiko Thieme. It is very rare to find a manager who beats indexes most years.

Sure, once in a while a manager comes along who beats the average and justifies higher costs. But this kind of manager is very difficult to find. And, when you do, he or she is often past the peak performance or you have to pay a fortune to obtain his or her services.

So one often ends up overpaying when one seeks out the latest investment superstar. You are paying for past, not future, successes. Most of the time, the star manager, charging premium costs, disappoints.

Lower costs are why the high-priced funds so often lose to the plain vanilla funds. In the final analysis, writes John Bogle, it is not alchemy, but cost efficiency that drives the index advantage. [See "The Triumph of Indexing" by John Bogle. This is just one of Bogle's many good books for the individual investor. I would also recommend Bogle's "Commonsense on Mutual Funds."].

Wayne Wagner, in his book, offers readers a secret. Anyone can become a millionaire.

How?

Wayne Wagner's Lunch Recommendations

Start early. Pack a lunch, he says.

"Take a few hundred dollars a month, the amount you spend on 30 lunches a month, and invest your money every month in a good index fund. That's it!" [From "Millionaire. The best explanation of how an index fund can turn your lunch money into a fortune." Wayne Wagner and Al Winnikoff.

Wagner offers numerous examples of how it works, but let's take one. Say you put $300 a month into an index fund. That's about 75 dollars a week or a little under eleven dollars a day. You earn nine percent a year, about an average rate of return for the stock market, and invest for 30 years. You have $553,000.

But say you do it for ten more years, 40 years. Then you have $1.414 million. Those extra ten years on top of the 30 years were stupendous. That's why Wagner, and almost every other sensible investment advisor, emphasizes "start early."

By the way, these wonderful numbers don't include investment taxes. But, as we will show below, your investments will take less of a hit if you are in an index fund as opposed to a managed mutual fund, where every trade—and managed funds trade a lot—can trigger a tax bill.

Less Is Better

Part of why most people tend to do better in an index fund over the long term than in a managed fund is the cost advantage. That's because you're too smart (stingy?) to give the tax man and the fat securities industry more than they usually get.

Let's compare the two. The average actively managed domestic equity fund, which trades a lot by buying and selling securities throughout the year, has a yearly expense ratio of about 1.4 percent. Buying and selling always requires expenses that are passed on to the investor. The higher the expense ratio, the more it hurts the fund's performance. The lower the expense ratio, the better the fund can perform.

However, the average domestic equity index fund, which changes a portfolio once a year based on an index it is trying to duplicate, is about 0.2 percent. Sometimes it can be as little as 0.1 percent. One caveat: Any so-called index funds that are not dirt cheap, which don't have expense ratios of around 0.2 percent or less, are trying to pull a fast one by invoking the good name of index funds, but offering something else.

The average index fund investor who refuses to overpay begins the year with at least 1.3 percent or 1.4 percent cost advantage over the investor who is paying for an actively managed fund.

The mistake you make by buying an average-cost mutual fund is that the average cost is "mind bogglingly" expensive, Blodget writes. [The Wall Street Self-Defense Manual."

Blodget should know. He often palmed off his company's pricey funds on clients when index funds were better performers.

Recently I had one other illustration of why index funds are generally better than managed funds. Close to my new home in Pittsburgh, there's a gentleman in a million-dollar home who is a quant for a major investment bank. He has access to the most elaborate investment formulas. I could not resist asking him how he invests his money. "Oh, I put my money in index funds. I use an S&P 500 trust fund." This gentleman is not throwing away his money on a high priced investment, he knows that spending two percent more than you must on investments can make a huge difference over the long run.

The mistake can cost an average of as much as two percent a year in returns. For example, Vanguard, surveying the returns of a Vanguard S&P 500 Portfolio index fund against the average domestic equity fund over the long term found the index fund won. The index returned 14 percent a year compared to 12.2 percent against the average domestic equity fund that was so much more expensive. The difference was 1.8 percent.

But it was worse. The study didn't include the managed funds' sales charges. Any reputable index fund has no sales charges, which are fees you pay to enter or leave a fund as well as higher investment taxes. So I think it is fair to say that the difference between the cheap as you know what index fund and the high-priced fund, the managed domestic equity fund that runs up big bills, is at least two percent a year over the long term.

Two Percent Can Equal a Fortune

Now some skeptical readers may be asking: Who cares? Isn't two percent a year an insignificant amount?

Over the short term, the answer is yes. However, a two percent difference over the long term, 10, 20 or 30 years, is an incredible amount. It can be an amount that can make dreams come true or it means disappointment because one didn't accumulate quite enough. Let's look at an example.

Bob Spend Big puts $300 a month into his managed funds. He uses pricey funds with high expense ratios. He earns seven percent a year. After 20 years, he has some $157,000. And after 30 years, he has $368,000. That sounds good, right? It's lousy compared to what he might have done had he carefully shopped for funds.

John Don't Waste Money also puts $300 a month into his funds, but they are low priced index funds. He earns not seven percent, but nine percent a year. After twenty years, he has $201,000. And after thirty years, he has $553,000, some $185,000 more than Bob. After 40 years, the disparity is even greater, Bob has $1.414 million compared to John's $792,000.

John, after forty years of investing and refusing to waste money, has some $622,000 more than Bob, who overpaid for his funds. By the way, Bob ends up farther ahead than that because we are not figuring in the taxes.

Index funds tend to incur less in investment taxes because they trade less than managed funds, which are buying and selling stocks frequently. Here's something many mutual fund companies don't tell you: Each time one sells an asset, one can run up a tax bill that the fund company passes on to the investor along with its management funds and only God knows what other costs passed on to the unsuspecting investor.

Here's an example: I used to go to a lot of luncheon/dinner events staged by mutual fund companies. Sometimes their would-be entertainment along with free bags of various goodies as part of the let's take care of the press approach. One firm once offered me a World Series ticket "at face value" for the sixth game of the 1996 World Series. (The face value of those tickets had skyrocketed by game six of that World Series. If you wanted a ticket by the night of the game you would have been paying three- or four-times face value). I watched it at home. My beloved Yankees closed out the Braves and won the series. I often thought, who was paying for this care and feeding of the press? Can you guess?

By the way, I once went to an event for the launching of a John Bogle book. They didn't offer me a cup of coffee. When

I asked for some water, a person informed me that there was a water fountain down the hall.

Index funds avoid so many expenses and Bob understood this. He was frugal, and, because he invested month after month in good times and bad, he ended up with much more than John. So, for those who say two percent doesn't matter, I ask: Would you rather be Bob or John?

The answer to that question may seem unimportant right now. But some day, when you're in your 50s or 60s or just sick of work in general or of a certain job with an obnoxious jefe, and you want to achieve financial independence so you can leave, the answer to that question might be the difference between a happy and an unhappy rest of your life.

This is not exaggeration. I know several people in their 60s who continue to work almost every day and go into Manhattan on the wretched, government run, New York City subways. By the way, the word wretched is not an exaggeration even though New York Governor Andrew Cuomo once said New Yorkers should be "proud" of their subways. I don't know anyone who "proudly" and happily rides the subways on a regular basis (Our ruling class leaders who have their own cars and keep away from mass transit don't).

Why is it so important to be among the Bobs and not the Johns?

Johns don't have enough in savings and must continue to earn a living. Maybe their primary income is from Social Security, which doesn't provide an adequate retirement income unless it is supplemented by large private income. And Social Security's skimpy payments could be under attack as we will learn in a later chapter.

Now that we have a plan to accumulate a large amount of assets over the long term, significant assets that can improve the quality of your life, it's time to stop and think about something that can ruin that plan. It is the problem of getting dazzled by the latest fashion in investing. It is the problem of choosing the short term over the long term. It is a mistake that many investors make who are looking for a short cut to immediate financial independence.

Chapter 12

Chasing the Hot Fund, How the average investor fails

That hot fund you just bragged about buying is unlikely to continue doing so well. Indeed, we saw in the last chapter the sad record of the long-gone American Heritage Fund, the ultimate hot and cold performer of funds.

The hot fund of this year has about a one in twelve chance of repeating outstanding performance next year. That's the warning of investment pros They see a constant pursuit of the newest investment stars by star struck investors. The average investor often chases last year's hot fund. But that fund rarely repeats top performance, leading to disappointed investors.

"Investors should be wary of the hot fund," says Richard Bernstein, a longtime money manager with his own advisory firm.

Let's Look at the Record

S&P in a recent report examining a three-year period, documented how the hot fund idea is dangerous.

"At the end of the first year in September 2017, there were 545 funds considered to be top quartile. By the following year in Sept. 2018, just under 47% of those funds remained in the top quartile, and by the end of the third year, in Sept. 2019, only 8% were still in the top quartile," according to the report by S&P Dow Jones Indices.

Nevertheless, many investors continue making the same mistake. They are jealous when they see friends and neighbors rack up big numbers one year, or who say they have gotten great numbers. Then they chase performance, a market researcher warns.

"They look at one year or three-year performance and make decisions based on that and that is the wrong way to do it," says Aye M. Soe, one of report's authors. Successful investors, she says, take a long-term view.

"One to three years is not enough," she explains. "Look at five to ten years and look at the consistency of the fund. Has it outperformed over the long term?"

Once a Star, Now You're a Bum

This year's stars could be next year's bums. In fact, it is possible this year's champs will be in the gutter next year. That's because this year a manager might not have been brilliant; the manager might just have been lucky but next year the luck could run out, Bernstein adds.

The fund manager, he argues, "simply exposed the portfolio the most to what worked. That in no way means the underlying exposures will work in the future," according to Bernstein.

Even a well-meaning regulation sometimes can feed this hot fund mania.

"Those required one-year performance numbers, numbers that fund companies often prominently advertise, can mislead the investor," warns Louis Harvey, president and chief executive officer of market observer Dalbar. He says companies are required to post one-year numbers.

Bad Numbers

But beware, he adds, sometimes numbers can mislead. The investor who seeks the hot investment by getting in and out of funds, can ruin a long-term return.

"In 2018 the average investor underperformed the S&P 500 in both good times and bad, lagging behind the S&P by more than 100 basis point in two different months," according to a Dalbar study.

One hundred basis points is one percent and one percent can be a lot over the long term.

"In October, a bad month for the market (-6.84% S&P 500 return vs. -7.97% Avg. Equity Investor Return) the investor lagged by 113 basis points, while in August, a strong month for the market (+3.26% S&P 500 return vs. 1.80% Avg. Equity Investor Return), the Average Investor lagged by 146 basis points," Dalbar said.

What should the investor do?

Ignore dazzling, often well-advertised, short-term numbers, pros say.

Seek more than one year of strong returns. Expect consistency over a long term. How has the fund performed in bad times as well as good?

Harvey says examine fund performance over five or ten non-consecutive years. See what it did in relation to funds in the same category and against appropriate market yardsticks, one of which could be the S&P 500.

Look for the fund that does well in the marathon, not one that just won the sixty-yard dash.

In the next section, we'll examine more self-destructive

practices. We'll discuss how one can borrow one's self into disaster.

Section 2: Protecting the Financial Independence It Took You Years to Build

Chapter 13

Easy Credit, The Servant that One Day Could Become a Brutal Master

"Just one percent lets you drive it away," Guardian Angels head Curtis Sliwa, pitching cars on television.

We've discussed this earlier. But we must discuss it again because of the critical importance of the subject to one's financial—and mental—health credit—how one views it and uses it in the course of a lifetime. It's important to use it wisely when you have money. It's critical to use it wisely when you're trying to build assets. It's important wherever you are in life. That's because if you don't use credit carefully, you'll likely never have any significant assets. You'll be too busy paying off cards.

I'll provide card some tips in this chapter that, if followed, will save one perhaps, tens of thousands of dollars of needless costs over the average lifetime.

First, consider the car sales pitch by Curtis Sliwa outlined at the top of this chapter.

Do you know what he means by "just one percent?"

It doesn't mean the car dealer is giving you a special deal and cutting the price of the car by 99 percent. It means, as with more and more big-ticket purchases of things like cars, houses and big screen TVs, that sellers today are often so motivated that they sell with less and less of a down payment.

But less and less of a down payment means more and more of a purchase must be paid for with credit. It means a much higher price. I've known people paying for a second car when they had yet to pay off the first!

That takes away more money from you. It is money that could have gone toward investments and making you financially independent. This easy credit, string out the loan over a long period, is a different way of paying for things than was used in prior generations.

Indeed, when our grandparents—many of whom had the sensibilities of smart investors because they went through hard times that few of us have—bought a car or a house, they put down a large chunk, perhaps 50 percent, of the purchase price. Then they financed the rest, which in this example was 50 percent. Sometimes they saved up and paid the entire price of a big item.

But, of course, Curtis Sliwa, who is paid by the car dealer because the dealer believes his celebrity pitch will increase sales, wants you to have a better deal than what your grandparents did.

Sure.

Financing Follies

Sliwa wants you to finance the car with 99 percent borrowed money. In the course of a three-or-four-year deal, the financing—the interest you pay on the borrowed money—might end up costing more than the car itself. The financing, the loan you use to buy the car, might go on longer than you have the car.

Credit lesson One: Go easy on financing. Maybe even avoid it altogether if you can. But if you must, buy cars with as little borrowed money as possible. Try to pay off the car as soon as possible. When you look back on a car you had for five or six years, you shouldn't conclude that the biggest expense of the car was the loan.

How different is this than the practices of our grandparents?

I was born in the 1950s. I can remember back when people would buy used cars with one hundred percent cash. That's why they bought used cars. You will notice, Dear Reader, that I dislike the euphemism "pre-owned." This term is an Orwellian Newspeak invention of car dealers trying to meet sales quotas.

Unlike new cars, they could pay for used cars on the spot and never have to worry about financing. That's something I did in the fall of 1978 when I moved to Indiana from New York and worked in small market radio. I bought my first car, a used VW Beetle. I just barely had enough, but I paid for it with cash. I had no car or credit card payments to make. I was happy about that. Back then, just paying for housing and food could be a challenge.

It was a great economical car that kept going in the worst weather. I was grateful. This was at a time when I was making very little. I couldn't afford credit card payments each month. I had enough trouble just paying for rent, taxes and food. (By the way, I was very lucky. Consider the young people who followed me in the 1980s. Many were also making small salaries but they often had huge student loans to pay).

The point is financing and all credit should be used only when needed and carefully. If overused, the credit or the financing becomes expensive, driving up the item's price.

An exception can be made in the case of financing an asset that can gain, not lose, in value, such as a house or a business. These are items in which the price can be reduced because of tax breaks and which often later, under the best of circumstances, can sometimes be sold for a profit. Nevertheless, whether buying a house in an up-and-coming neighborhood or a business that one expects will provide a living, one should be careful to avoid excessive debt.

But in the case of a car, pre-owned (sic) or otherwise, unless one has a very rare car, the value of an auto almost always will start to decline when one takes possession. The use of credit to buy fun things, things that would be difficult to sell such as TVs and other consumer items, should be approached the way one would walk through a dangerous neighborhood at night—very carefully, with the understanding that so many bad things can happen and one should move as fast as possible. The bad neighborhood of personal finance for many is the credit card.

The Worst Way to Borrow

Credit cards are the most expensive way to access credit outside of loan sharks and Mafia Dons.

Why?

The credit card is an "unsecured" debt. People who don't understand the economics of the product don't understand that this is why card interest rates are so high. Unlike a house or a car, where when the loan fails the bank can take back the house or the car, there is nothing backing the card other than a promise to pay. Millions have broken promises to card companies both in bad and good times.

This kind of loan is often quite risky and card companies often write off billions in bad loans each year although I'm not running any testimonial dinners for the credit card companies. The quality of these dicey loans is priced into the card. So credit cards have very high interest rates.

It is a kind of loan that some people use to pay that one percent for a car or for so many "must have now" purchases.

Yet many of these purchases could be delayed until they could be paid for without debt.

These credit card junkies carry credit balances from month to month. They begin to run the race of trying to pay for all manner of things at the same time with a 20 percent interest rate slapped on top of their purchases.

Lesson Two: Repeat this promise and mean it: "I will carry as little or no credit card debt from month-to- month, even if it means delaying luxury purchases for a few months or even a year or so." (Notice the pledge doesn't cover necessities, such as food, clothing and shelter).

Pledge to become a transactor, not a revolver. Revolvers are people who think Curtis Sliwa is doing them a favor when he raves about only one percent and you can drive it away.

Transactors are smart investors. Transactors are detested by credit card companies. Transactors are people like me and my wife today although in the early years of our marriage we did carry some card debt until we realized how we were hurting ourselves and stopped. Today we only buy things that we can pay off in one credit card cycle. We became transactors, a curse word in much of the credit card industry.

Who are transactors?

They are people who borrow and make the other guy, the big credit card company, pay.

They are smart people who get their credit card bills each month and pay them off in their entirety.

Transactors are smart. They are saving big money over the long term because they don't put down one percent and finance the rest over years and years. They pay zero percent on their card charges. They are sticking it to the card industry and many executives in the business hate their guts. They take money out of their pockets. They are making the card companies give them short term zero percent interest loans. They are making the card companies pay through the nose.

Credit card company executives detest them. I know because I once worked for a publication that covered the credit card industry. I often spoke to officials of credit card issuers. There are various curse words that card executives use when they refer to hated transactors. I can't repeat them because I am an old man of delicate disposition.

So why don't card companies end the zero percent interest loan? Some would like to do so but there is the problem of competition. There's lot of it in the card industry. They also need transactors in order to find the suckers, I mean revolvers. Sometimes smart people start doing stupid things and card issuers love when that happens.

Still, from time to time there have been discussions within the credit card industry of ending the transactor bargain; of discontinuing the grace period and assessing interest on a card from the moment a purchase is made. But those discussions seem to get about as far as the average pol once in a while advocating that the government spend less money. He thinks about it for about five seconds. Then he returns to his or her glorious dreams of big government spending and getting relatives, flunkies and political allies on the public payroll.

The problem for them but not for you is the card industry eats it young and everyone else that isn't moving fast. If some card issuers ended the grace period, others would start screaming that they would never end the grace period. This would be a way of stealing business; that they still wanted all transactors to know their business was welcome. Competition, the brilliant economist Milton Friedman once argued, is the greatest consumer protection.

How much do transactors save? A boatload of money over a long period. And, like the power of compounding in investing, the sooner one starts, the better.

The Perpetual Debt

Let's assume one carries $20,000 in credit card debt at 20 percent interest. Over the course of a year that's $4,000 just in interest on the debt. If you just pay the interest you still have a $20,000 debt at the end of year. You haven't touched principal.

Remember that bill mess is all yours. The government won't let you take off any of the interest on your taxes as it once did until the late 1980s when the tax code was changed.

Four thousand dollars a year over ten years is $40,000. Over thirty years that's $120,000. That's all because you understood that the Curtis Sliwas of the world were not doing you any favors. And by the way, there are other benefits besides the $120,000.

Because you pay off your bills quickly, you have a sterling credit record. Card issuers will rush to give you the best deals—cards with no annual fees and all sorts of goodies. You will get more rebate points, which can translate into bigger cash refunds. You might get a few hundred dollars back in rebate cash. The total savings of all these card practices are huge. They go on and on for the rest of your life as long as you follow these sensible practices.

Maybe beyond your personal finances, you can educate others on the virtues of being a transactor. Remember most young people don't get this kind of education in school or even at home if their parents know little about finance. Yes, like alcoholism, financial mismanagement can be passed from one generation to another. The clever Investor can defeat the card companies and can break that destructive cycle.

Here's another benefit of using a credit card sensibly. When you purchase a house, your banker will look up your credit history. When he sees it, he won't make a face and say you haven't got a chance to get a mortgage. Instead, the banker will say you have top credit. The banker will ask you to sit in the best chair and have a cup of coffee. He'll start acting like a young single man when a super model comes his way. The banker will want to offer you the bank's products.

Transactors will also have better mental health and sleep better than many others who live in fear that their creditors are going to seize their assets. That's because no one will call you at all hours of the day and night to dun you.

Bothersome Barristers

And when those late-night tube ads come on for those sleazy solicitors who tell desperate people far behind in their card payments that "bankruptcy is not an end; it is a new beginning," you'll dismiss them as the ambulance chasing sleazebags some are.

An aside: I wonder how many of those lawyers whooping it up for bankruptcy filings, who seem to think bankruptcy is like a Sunday walk in the park, have had to file for bankruptcy themselves? They're like pols who lecture you that you must use mass transit but use cars to get around.

Paying your bills means you'll be able to shake your head when those tube ads pollute the airwaves and know that's not you. (I'll have a chapter later on devoted to some of those fly-by night schemes that can supposedly get you out of credit card hell without having to pay back your debts). You'll know that no one will be calling you in the middle of the night demanding payment.

But the wise person will save as much as six figures during a lifetime because this person insists on living as a transactor.

There's a lot of good reasons for these sensible practices, but I can think of one now: Isn't it difficult enough to earn an extra $120,000?

Do yourself, do your spouse, do your family a big favor: Learn how to spend and use credit cards wisely. Learn how to pay your bills each month. Mute the tube when ads for "pre-owned" cars come on.

However, let's assume that you haven't followed these principles. You face hard choices. You can't pay your credit card bills. What now?

Chapter 14

A Road Out of Card Hell? Beware the Card Settlement Companies

You're in credit card debt. You're in so deep you're considering bankruptcy.

Wait a minute, did you know that you don't have to pay it all back?

Really?

Well, that's what a television announcer claims. He speaks in such soothing tones. It's as though he is letting you—and only you—in on this great secret that will save you a fortune.

There's "a secret that the credit card companies don't want you to know."

This so-called "secret" will allow you to wipe out card debts for a fraction of what you owe.

So begins a commercial for a credit card settlement company. The announcer says anyone with $5,000 or more of card debt can call. These kinds of companies claim that they can pull you out of your debt mess on the cheap.

The Card Settlement Company Pitch

"On average, we save our clients in excess of 55% of what they otherwise would owe," says Rick Burton, executive vice president with Credit Associates.

"Negotiating with creditors directly can be a difficult and laborious process, which is why many people turn to professional debt settlement companies like Freedom Debt Relief," says Michael Micheletti, a company spokesman.

Depending on the customer, Freedom Relief can reduce a debt by about half, he says. Customers, he adds, pay a fee, often about 15 percent, based on the amount of the debt reduced.

Micheletti cites an example. Say the company, with the cardholder's approval, negotiates a $20,000 reduction in a person's card debt. Then the fee would be $3,000, according to Micheletti.

How Can They Do It?

Card companies try to collect on an unsecured asset, say credit card industry experts. However, unlike a mortgage on a home, there's no asset to seize when one can't pay, often making it difficult to collect anything. Card companies, which now have record business because so many Americans never learned the financial values of their grandparents, are often ready to negotiate bad debts, some card industry experts say.

Card settlement companies claim they'll get a good deal for overextended cardholders, a better deal than you could. But now it's my turn to play the role of not so soothing announcer: Credit card experts and regulators question debt settlement services and their methods.

Debt settlement companies ask a cardholder to transfer an agreed on amount every month into an escrow-like account, according to a paper by the Federal Trade Commission (FTC). The amount is enough to pay off a settlement that is reached with the card company. "Further, these programs often encourage or instruct their clients to stop making any monthly payments to their creditors," FTC wrote.

But the FTC warns some debt settlement companies are scams. For example, the FTC moved against 11 debt settlement companies in Florida.

Taking Your Money and Doing Nada

"Overtime," the FTC wrote, "victims found their debts unpaid, their accounts in default and their credit scores damaged."

Some companies, the FTC says, "may try to collect their own fees from you before they have settled any of your debts—a practice prohibited under the FTC's Telemarketing Sales Rule (TSR) for companies engaged in telemarketing these services."

A credit card industry analyst, who says he would never recommend these services, complains even legitimate ones don't advertise the downside.

"Settling your debt for less than you owe has a devastating effect on your credit. FICO says someone with excellent credit (a 780 score) could lose 140-160 points due to debt settlement," says Ted Rossman, with CreditCards.com.

"That would put them on the verge of a subprime score," he adds. "They would find it harder and more expensive to obtain future credit, and the negative effects could last for years."

Credit Associates' Burton agrees that one's credit score will be hurt: "As we tell all clients "Participation in our program will most likely continue to hurt their credit score in the short term. Once debt is resolved, however, they may work on improving that score."

Freedom Debt Relief's Micheletti adds that, in many cases,

"our prospective clients are not in a position to be seeking credit and, therefore, are better off to address their underlying debt problems and then work with us to rebuild their credit scores."

There's another issue; an issue that I have never seen advertised on those late-night ads aimed at desperate people. Any amount forgiven is treated as income and taxed, according to Bernard Kiely, a CPA in Morristown, New Jersey. "You'll get a 1099 form on that," he says.

Credit card settlement companies don't dispute this but insist their services are needed.

Burton concedes that there are some "disreputable" card settlement companies. Still, he says Credit Associates provides an important service and it isn't paid until there is a satisfactory settlement.

"We deliver exactly what we promise," he says.

There are lots of potential candidates for these services. Americans are setting new card debt levels. Indeed, in a recent poll, millions of Americans conceded that their debts were unlikely to be paid in their lifetimes.

I'll never escape my debts. I'll take them to my grave.

That's the lament of millions of Americans, according to a CreditCards.com study.

About two thirds of American adults polled, don't know when or if they will ever be debt free, the study said. This includes 25 percent of those polled who expect to take debts to the grave.

The average household had a card debt of $8,169 in November 2018, or about $1.042 trillion dollars, according to the Federal Reserve. The Fed added the $1.042 trillion figure exceeded the previous pre-recession credit card record of

$1.02 trillion in 2008.

An adviser warns that many cardholders, running up record debt, need to think twice about their debts.

"These people who believe that they will die in debt need a change in attitude. They need to sit down with someone who will help them get out of the debt trap," according to Charles Hughes, a certified financial planner in Bay Shore, New York. Hughes is skeptical about credit card settlement companies.

A Way Out

Still, there is a way out of card hell.

"The most common strategy," according to the study, "is paying substantially more than the minimum monthly payment."

Rossman, the industry analyst with CreditCards.com., says "I advise people that they can get out of debt, but it won't be easy."

Rossman believes paying much more than the minimum makes sense. He also says non-profit credit card counseling firms can also help.

Most professional advisors recommend non-profit credit counselors. Rossman likes Money Management International.

But there is one other reasonable option other than card settlement services but, if you take it, you must be disciplined and stick to the strategy: zero percent balance transfer cards can also help, Rossman adds.

These cards, he adds, can give "people a pause from paying a card debt that can include some 25 percent interest for those with the worst credit records."

However, the disadvantage of these zero percent cards is

some people use the respite from interest on old debt to run up new debts. Some of these zero percent cards, Rossman notes, charge a fee for transferring debt.

Each of these cards, Rossman says, offer 15 months with 0% interest and no transfer fees. Some zero percent transfer cards, he adds, can offer longer periods of zero percent interest—up to 21 months—but charge 3% to 5% transfer fees.

Some of these specific cards might not be available so you might have to look elsewhere. Do a net search for zero percent cards. Go to card monitoring sites such as LowCards .com. or CreditCards.com. Remember, when you get a zero percent deal, the clock is running, often for only six to 18 months. You must become debt free, or as close to debt free, as soon as possible. Pay as much as you can every month, then see if you find a little more.

Use that period to get rid of your debts. Otherwise, at the end of the grace period, you'll be in deeper than ever and more likely to listen to those looney lawyers with the bankruptcy spiels.

To avoid ever having to face these difficult situations or to get out of them as fast as possible remember the basic money management principles that I have advocated.

Let me repeat the credit card advice that never changes. Become a transactor, not a revolver, as soon as possible.

Revolvers, people who are committing financial suicide. They should stop doing so as soon as possible.

What's to Be Done?

I can see why people use card debt settlement companies. They seem to offer a way out of a hopeless situation.

Still, in most cases the secondary damage they do—wrecking your credit rating and generating additional tax money for our Potomac pals, who always seem desperate for more money—mean one should avoid debt settlement services or only use them as a last resort.

Better than that, if you think you're starting to get in too deep in credit card hell, take action now. Pay off card debt as fast as possible. Early in our marriage, my wife and I once got in as deep as $4,000 in card hell and then we yelled, "basta ya!"

We spent a good deal less over three months and were debt free. We never used a debt settlement service and never incurred more taxes. We did it ourselves through spending discipline.

So make sacrifices now and you will be rewarded later.

Chapter 15

Grey Charges Can Cost You a Bundle

Another Few Hundred Dollars Are Blowing by You---Why Don't You Reach Over and Pick Them Up?

Wise investors understand that what you don't know can and often will hurt you.

For instance, do you know who is reaching into your credit card accounts and adding new charges?

Check your credit card bills. Plenty of sleazy merchants would like to pick your pocket. Indeed, if not careful, some $215 or more in unauthorized charges could be added on to your bill every year.

So it's not only important to keep your credit card spending under control, you should be sure that others aren't taking advantage of you through a scheme called grey charges.

What are they?

Grey charges are assessed against unsuspecting cardholders for things they have not said that they want. They are not illegal, but are unethical. They are socking millions of people each year with bills they never authorized. It's possible you already have been affected. You must be vigilant in watching out for these charges.

Indeed, unscrupulous merchants, using the convenience of the credit card information you provide, are grabbing lots of extra money out of the pockets of unsuspecting consumers. Grey charges can even strike a person who believes he or she has sense and doesn't need to check credit card accounts more than once in a while. Grey charges are costing consumers billions of dollars a year in charges they never approved.

Billions of Dollars Out the Window

Credit card holders are losing some billions of dollars each year—a recent estimate was some $14 billion—to grey, or deceptive, credit or debit-card charges, according to a study by securities industry consultant Aite Group. That's not chopped liver. Indeed, it amounts to $215 a year per cardholder on charges like a cancelled gym membership or an unsubscribed magazine or some service that has been renewed without your knowledge or approval.

Companies exercising their grey rights (however wrong they may seem to many of us) are well-known entities that many of us do business with every day.

They know levying charges is legal, but unethical, according to fraud expert Robert Siciliano.

Grey charges, the report says, are a problem for the card companies. They are also losing money on them as well as enraging customers.

Why?

Because issuers incur service-related expenses when cardholders question and dispute charges, the report says.

"I would estimate that it is costing the card companies some $360 million more a year in costs than the additional revenue that comes through their network", said Aite Group analyst Ron Shevlin, the author of the report, which is entitled "The Economic Impact of Grey Charges on Debit and Credit Card

Issuers."

Banks don't want grey charges and the administrative problems they bring. They lead to unhappy customers who cancel their cards, explains Nessa Feddis, a senior vice president for consumer protection and payments for the American Bankers Association.

Let's look at an example of how these grey charges trick people. Let's look at what happened to me.

I read the Wall Street Journal. I believe it is an outstanding paper. Nevertheless, some of the people running its subscriptions department are the kind of people who, if they visit your house, you should check to see if your silverware and other valuables are still around.

I was offered a discounted six months subscription to the Wall Street Journal and I jumped on it. I paid by supplying my credit card number. About five months into the subscription, the subscription service, using my card information, automatically renewed my subscription for a year and at the premium rate. Now I would pay a much higher charge than I was initially offered and one I surely would have rejected if I had known what was going on. But now they were assessing my card a big new charge. By the way, this is why, when you subscribe, they refuse payment by check. The latter means you make a new payment and might re-consider. The card charges can be automatically renewed.

What's This?

Once I saw this new charge online—and I tend to look at my card accounts a few times a week—I went ballistic. I had some questions for these subscriber people, eager to start charging my card. Who said I wanted to renew at that rate?

I didn't.

Who said I wanted to use that same card again, since I now had a new card that offered better rebate points?

I didn't.

How was the subscription service able to do this in the first place?

Well, many times, when one subscribes to a magazine or some other service, the agreement will contain a fine print clause that says the subscription automatically renews unless you take action.

I cancelled the new, more expensive, subscription and had the subscription service officials remove the bill from my card account. I threatened to alert the fraud division of the card company if they didn't revoke the charge.

They did. Pronto. By the way, since that time the Wall Street Journal has tried to get me back by offering, once again, a wonderful introductory rate. I signed on again, but I didn't give them my credit card. I wrote a check for the introductory offer. The Journal wasn't interested. They are only interested in getting your credit card number and living for the day when they can automatically renew you at a higher rate. That's something they can't do if you pay by check.

Given the premium rate the Wall Street Journal had tried to impose on me, I was better off buying the paper at the newsstand a few times a week.

You can survive by buying other things, by always being aware of competitors principle is something to remember when dealing with prickly merchants. They think they can control you by threatening you with a cutoff of their precious goods or services.

But unlike the government with its persistent taxes, no one can force you into buying products or services. That's barring the oasis owner in the middle of the Sahara who has the only source of water that would be the difference between life and death.

Excepting the oasis example, you allow yourself to buy the product. In effect, you often force yourself, sometimes out of laziness, by not insisting that your money belongs to you.

Today, thanks in part to the net, there are so many more ways to buy different things than there were before. Exercise choice. In my case, while I still read the Wall Street Journal sometimes, I also find other sources for good business reporting and analysis. Make people earn your business and not take it for granted. Some pushy merchants believe that consumers are cattle that can be herded anywhere. Don't let them do it to you.

So grey charges are not illegal, but nevertheless many people end up buying services they didn't want or for a period they never agreed to—such in my case trying to force me to buy an extra year on my newspaper subscription.

Some card issuers, Shevlin says, are considering providing apps that would identify a grey charge. Still, he concedes that is not going to happen soon. Until that happens, frequent monitoring is the best strategy in avoiding or reversing such charges.

Check Your Bills Frequently

Consumers should look at their card bills each month, Shevlin adds. I would say each week or perhaps several times a week. There's a lot of chicanery on the net. They should read disclosure agreements. It is amazing how many consumers don't take these common-sense steps.

Wise investors have common-sense. Thanks to electronic records, you can check your credit and debit card records as often as you wish. Of course, one must pay for everything one authorizes with a debit or credit card. However, there is no reason to pay bogus or grey charges.

Remember, the card companies want your patronage because the business is very competitive. They want happy customers who will charge lots of things so they can make more money. They don't want angry customers dropping a card because there are lots of other places to go for credit cards. Remember, as we have said, to charge only what you can pay off each month and avoid interest.

Each card association, such as Visa and MasterCard, has big fraud divisions. These associations want to hear about complaints from clients who are upset about devious merchants using their networks. They will stop charges that are dubious and investigate.

Sometimes they don't know what is going on. They don't want angry cardholders who, if they believe they are being charged unfairly, will also blame them and their members, the banks that issue the cards. Their cardholders will take their business elsewhere, which is easy to do. Regulators will eventually ask why their card networks were being used unethically.

Remember, even if some merchants or card companies don't respond to your complaints, you, the investor, have the ultimate power. Cancel the card and get another. Assuming you have a decent payment record, you have almost limitless choices in obtaining credit.

The smart investor has a permanent interest in getting the best deal and not getting cheated by merchants—today, tomorrow and for as long as he or she spends money. He or she also knows how important it is to protect those assets and how taxes can destroy them.

Once you have accumulated the assets to make you comfortable for the rest of your life, it is also very important to know how to protect them. Uncle Whiskers and his relentless horde of publicans are ever hungry to grab your geld. It's important, once you have some, to know how to protect it. Let's assume you've followed much of the advice here and are independent or almost independent. How do you protect it?

Chapter 16

Effective Retirement Strategies, Some Assets Are More Valuable than Others.

Let's consider a person we haven't looked at in detail: Someone who has accumulated considerable assets—enough so he or she hopes to last for the rest of a life—and a lot of them are in retirement accounts.

Now there is a new problem to solve because money, the same as health, requires perpetual attention. When you have them, you must guard them. That's because both are very easy to lose. Both are difficult to recover.

Indeed, if your assets drop to dangerous levels in retirement, it is very difficult. That's because your prime earning years are behind you. It is unlikely that you will ever want to go back to full-time work. Whoever wants to go back to driving that horrid freeway at rush hour ten times a week or squeezing on that egregious E-train again? So the point of this chapter is to ensure you never face such a problem.

How does one preserve the assets, which can be easily used or excessively taxed, leaving you with little or nothing in your last years? Advisors offer various commonsense strategies.

Spend taxable assets first. Protect qualified assets as long as possible. That's because their tax advantaged status makes them golden. That is general advice of most retirement advisors. They say there are exceptions to this rule, but not a lot.

Why give preferred status to qualified assets?

These investments, those investments qualifying for deferred taxation, can be wonderful for retirees and those saving for retirement. Taking maximum advantage of these retirement accounts—such as traditional IRAs, 401(k)s among and Roth IRAs among others—is a big part of attaining and preserving wealth.

Will You Outlast Your Money?

In most cases, you can start spending your qualified money without penalty beginning at age 59.5. Before that, unless you have a medical emergency or some special circumstance, you will pay the investment taxes and penalties on tax of the taxes.

But, when you reach age 59.5, remember this: You are not required to start spending your qualified money. Whether or not you start spending at age 59.5 is a key decision in whether or not you will run out of money over the course of an average lifespan, which is increasing almost every year. However, this has implications for retirement planning: You must prepare for more years.

So remember one can wait until between ages 70 and 72 to begin collecting from qualified accounts (And Congress, as I write this, was considering it beyond age 72. If so, this would be a tax break that the average person should use). Many advisors say, depending on your circumstances, one should wait the extra 11 years or more before using qualified assets. Use taxable accounts first, they say. Later use qualified assets and, as much as possible, preserve them by letting them grow for a long period. In the meantime, use other assets first.

The often-effective strategy of spending taxable assets first in retirement and letting qualified assets continue to grow as long as possible is important in several respects. Advisers say that by delaying the use of these qualified accounts you can help yourself.

Remember, once one starts using them, one triggers investment taxes. For example, say you have $500,000 in an IRA and you are required to take out $50,000. Then the $50,000 is subject to taxation while the other $450,000 continues to compound. that year it was a bull market and the IRA account grew more than the withdrawal. So, you got your $50,000 and yet at the end of the year you still have $500,000. We can't assume that every year is a bull market since the stock market, long term, tends to go down one year out of three. However, the point of this preserve qualified assets as long as possible approach is this: The longer you can stay in the stock market, the more likely you are to catch more bull markets.

So the point of delaying the use of these assets as much as possible, or only taking a minimum distribution each year. This strategy extends the compounding process. That improves your margin of safety. This is sensible because the odds are most of us are going to give longer than we expect. That, and persistent inflation, means most of us will need more assets.

Keep Compounding

Compounding, at almost any age and in almost any situation, is your friend in achieving financial goals. It is a vital element in the creation and expansion of personal wealth. This is true whether one is trying to build a retirement nest egg or preserve it as long as possible.

The is why allowing qualified assets to grow as long as possible is often a critical factor in whether a retirement plan will succeed. That means ensuring your money outlasts you.

For instance, say one has $922,000 in a qualified retirement account. How did you get there?

You put $500 a month into the account and earned nine percent a year on average over the course of 30 years. However, say you don't access your money at age 59 when you can without penalty.

You leave it to compound another ten years or so. In fact, you take a part time job. Maybe make $6,000 or $7,000 a year. You can keep contributing $500 a month to your qualified account. You let it continue to grow, perhaps at the historic long-term return of the stock market. That's about nine percent a year. That extra decade was important to the compounding process and it will show up in your final balance.

In the meantime, you use taxable accounts to pay for your expenses. By the way, as you run down taxable assets, you tax bill declines because your investment taxes tend to decline. This happens at the same time as the value of your tax deferred accounts have likely risen over the decade.

A Lot More

Ten years later, again assuming the average nine percent a year average return, you have about 150 percent more in your qualified account. You have some $1.3 million more in qualified money (final balance some $2.2 million). That's because you didn't do what some people do: You didn't start taking distributions at age 59.5. and start paying taxes as soon as possible. That's an approach that most of the time is wrong, according to most advisers.

The point is: You can start taking distributions at age 59 without penalty but you are not required to do so. Don't do it unless you must to pay your bills.

By protecting tax-advantaged assets, you let the compounding continue and added to it. By the way, in the case of a Roth IRA, you never have to take a distribution. And, as long as you have earned income each year, say a part-time job in which you make $7,000 a year, you can continue to contribute all of it to your Roth account.

The strategy, for most people and in an average investment climate—the stock market tends to go up two out of three years over the long term—is very effective most of the time.

"That can mean an enormous increase in your retirement savings," says advisor Andrew Schwartz, a White Plains, New York advisor. He cautions that those retiring too early, who start taking money from qualified accounts from ages 60-65, could "be doing irreversible damage to the portfolio."

Another strategy, if you can use it, is to take minimum distributions from a qualified account. By doing this, one exposes oneself to lower taxation and allows some compounding to continue even when you are retired. Let's say you have $330,000 in a qualified account and your minimum distribution one year is about $12,000.

But say you want a little more. You take 150 percent more than the minimum distribution, some $30,000, and have to pay taxes on it. However, you still have $300,000 remaining in the qualified account that is still not being taxed.

If it is a good year and you earn 10 percent on the remaining balance, then, at the end of the year, you once again have $330,000 and had the benefit of $30,000. With some luck, smart management and decent markets, one's qualified accounts will never run out even if you live a very long time.

Again, this strategy is another example of why diversification is so important. Here we are talking about having both kinds of assets. This strategy only works if you also have taxable assets to access in the early part of retirement and are not dependent on the qualified assets. The latter should be pre-served as long as possible. By that I mean, retirement, in its ideal, is supposed to be wonderful; a time to do the things you always wanted to but never had the time or money to do before.

So one should have both kinds of assets—taxable and tax deferred—but the latter are very valuable and are often the most important element in achieving financial independence before or during retirement.

A Critical Approach

The strategy can be an essential part and maintaining a com-fortable retirement, according to advisors who specialize in retirement planning.

"The point of accessing qualified assets last is right on the mark. It is the smart thing to do," says Charles Hughes, a certified financial planner in Bay Shore, New York.

"We tend to delay the use of retirement assets as long as possible," adds Steve Branton, an advisor in San Francisco.

But some pre-retirees and retirees don't understand how important it is not only to accumulate enough in retirement assets but also to know how to use retirement accounts. These accounts have contribution and distribution rules. One can avoid a boatload of taxes over the course of a life-time through maximizing contributions before retirement, then employing an effective distribution strategy in retire-ment. This can be the difference between golden years or worrying about money in your last years.

"Distribution strategies actually start long before retire-ment," notes Melissa Brennan, an advisor in Plano, Texas. "The goal should be to lower the client's lifetime tax burden by triggering taxes mindfully in a way that lowers the client's lifetime tax bill."

This is a critical for millions of Americans, with a huge part of their wealth in qualified accounts (About 60 percent of our wealth is in qualified accounts. The latter have made us financially independent, but it took a few decades of compounding to reach it). Many Americans do the same. Indeed, by the middle of 2020, they had some $30 trillion in the various retirement accounts, according to the Investment Company Institute, the trade group of the mutual fund industry.

"As a general principle, with some exceptions, one should defer qualified assets as long as possible," says Boyan Doytchinov, an advisor in Medford, New York. "That is a good starting point in retirement planning."

Why?

You will be letting your qualified retirement accounts with their tax advantages grow for the maximum period. The more this compounding can take place, the better it is for your final retirement balances.

"When you start retirement planning early, you put a powerful force in your corner: time. The longer your money is invested, the more time it can compound," writes Matt Kranz in "Retirement Planning for Dummies."

Protecting qualified assets can also make a marked difference in a retirement nest egg.

The point may seem minor. However, the strategy is true both if one is in the last years of saving for retirement, or if one is in retirement and wants to ensure a comfortable level of assets is retained throughout retirement.

Saving Is Good

This, along with electing to save as much as possible for as long as possible, increases your chances of never running out of money. The strategy can also be extended by working a little longer through part-time work. Don't go straight into retirement if you're a little short on retirement funds or if you're not short of retirement assets but just bored by the idea of never working again. Part-time work, semi-retirement, could be the key decision of a successful plan.

"By and large, those who continue to work until their mid-60s or beyond should have a reasonably comfortable retirement," according to Alice H. Munnell, a retirement expert writing in the book "Working Longer: The Solution to the Retirement Income Challenge."

But sometimes the delayed or reduced use of qualified assets strategy has caveats.

For instance, a Long Island advisor cites an exception to the general rule of protecting the qualified assets.

"I have asked clients sometimes to consider using qualified funds in the first couple of years of retirement so that they can defer taking Social Security until a later age. Each year they wait between 62 and normal retirement age, their social security benefit increases by 8%," says John Carbonara of Jericho, New York. Waiting until age 70 to collect Social Security increases monthly payments by about 25 percent.

Doytchinov emphasizes that "there are no cookie cutter approaches to retirement planning that work every time." Sometimes, he adds, "it makes sense to take money from a Roth IRA early in retirement because it can keep you in a lower tax bracket."

The distributions from Roth IRAs, unlike traditional IRAs,

aren't counted in taxation. Still, he agrees that protecting and expanding qualified assets can be an effective approach to ensuring one never outlives assets.

(By the way, this approach needs the help of some the retirement planners we are quoting here. If you need an advisor, we have a chapter coming up on how to find one.

Always Overprepare

How one spends assets in retirement is important. It is because all retirement planning, no matter how effective, has some degree of uncertainty. So, in this chapter, we are using a principle advocated by World War II general Dwight Eisenhower: It is better to be overprepared; to have a more than you think you need for any battle, such as the battle to have adequate resources in one's retirement.

That's because, no matter how smart the advisor, all retirement plans have some unknowns. Every plan contains some assumptions, assumptions that could change or, in extreme cases, wreck a plan so one must be able to adjust.

By the way, President Eisenhower said that, since war was such a messy unpredictable business, that it was always sensible to have far more troops than you think you would need to accomplish a mission. That's because, no matter how good a plan, something will always go wrong in almost every plan, even the good ones. The same principle should apply to retirement planning. There are many factors that can change, factors that could wreck a retirement plan.

Let's Assume....

Indeed, one never knows how long a given amount of retirement money will need to last. That's because one doesn't know the exact number of retirement years.

You may live as long as your parents. Possibly, you won't, but the odds are you will live longer than you expect. Are you planning for 10 more years, 20, or even 30 years? Lifespan continues to increase and that needs to be calculated in drawing up a plan.

Part of constructing an effective plan also depends on the correct assumption of an inflation rate. Inflation is the government's slow or fast debasing of buying power based on how much money it creates. The government money presses have been going overtime. Inflation happens through the monetary policies of the central bank along with the spending policies of Congress and the president.

Government spending, as we see this year, tends to increase in election years. That's when people running for office tend to promise everything to voters to get their support.

Over the past century the debasement number, or inflation, rate has been about three percent a year on average in the United States. But that could be irrelevant in the case of a given retirement in a high inflationary period. For instance, many of our grandparents who retired ran into a horrible problem called stagflation, which was high inflation rates combined with a slow growth, or no growth, economy. They faced a buzzsaw of rising costs combined with poor returns on their retirement assets.

Indeed, there have been periods of high inflation such as in the 1970s when inflation was sometimes double digit. It was a horror show for people on fixed incomes; people who had a lot of their money in cash or low interest return bonds. Stocks, through much of this period, were also in the dumps. However, the last 10 to 15 years have been periods of low single digit inflation although now there are fears that double digit inflation will return. Will it? Better to heed Ike's counsel. Prepare for the worst.

Indeed, given the incredible deficits both right-wing and

left-wing governments have been rolling up, I think that a long period of high inflation might happen. Generally, high inflation is bad for stocks and can destroy a retirement plan.

Another retirement plan assumption will be how much can one project the return on your portfolio during a retirement. In the 1970s, for example, stock market returns were bad. There was a period of 1973-74 when the market went down by about 40 percent. You will want a retirement plan that can survive even if bad times begin just after you retire.

Since people live longer today—unlike our grandparents who often depended on low interest "safe" bonds and cash for retirement income in part because they didn't live as long as we do on average—many younger retirees in their 60s face unique problems. They could have twenty or maybe thirty or more years to go. Some will live to 100 or beyond. Will they have enough money to live comfortably?

These people living to an old age will need to hold at least some stocks longer than their grandparents did, many of whom lived comfortably from bond and certificate of deposit yields.

Many of today's younger retirees must have part of their portfolios in stocks. That's because stocks tend to provide the highest long-term rate of return of most investment categories. But, in exchange for the higher returns, they can also be a rocky ride. There are periods when stocks are bow wows.

In the first decade of the century, stocks underperformed. They were investment dogs. In the last decade they have been great; both under the Obama and Trump administrations. However, as I write this, there was a fear that we are on the verge of another bear market.

Indeed, a big money manager, Richard Bernstein, recently said we could be nearing a bear market. He may be wrong.

But the key, especially for young and middle-aged people with lots of years to invest, is not to worry about today's market but to invest for the long term. If we do enter into a bear market soon, remember you, young person, are in the stock market for long run. So, adopting the effective, invest every month in good times and bad, strategy, you should do well. But for the rest of us, time, the inability to have enough of it for our investments to recover from a bear market, could hurt us.

All of these factors into the question of if will one have enough in retirement savings?

"That's the $64,000 question," writes attorney and CPA James Lange in his book "Retire Secure. Pay Taxes Later." Lange. a longtime advisor in Pittsburgh, adds that, since there are many retirement variables, no plan can be 100 percent secure.

The dangers of poor retirement planning are considerable. Some people run out of assets. Others have assets that run down so much in their last years that their quality of life is diminished. They have little or nothing in savings, either qualified or non-qualified.

Indeed, millions of Americans have Social Security as their primary retirement income. But Social Security, the jewel in the crown of the American welfare state, on average only pays about $18,000 a year. However, as a write, the payment is due to increase because inflation has spiked. Still, Social Security's Trust fund has been running in the red for several years owing to mismanagement by right-wing and left-wing governments. In a recent Social Security Trust Fund report, the trustees wrote "reserves will become depleted in 2035."

What happens then?

If nothing changes, there will be a 20 percent cut in benefits, according to Social Security Chief Actuary Stephen Goss. In an interview I conducted with him for another publication, he told me "Congress will need to act."

Given these uncertainties, Social Security, at best, should be a small percentage of a retirement plan, advisors say. (For more on Social Security, please chapters, "Don't Overrely on Social Security" and a Q&A with Goss).

"When people plan on having 50 percent or more of their retirement income from Social Security, it is difficult for me to write an effective retirement plan," Hughes warns.

What's the Plan?

So, to avoid that, one needs effective strategies in accumulating and maintaining qualified assets, often the most important part of pre-retiree and retiree portfolios.

But Lange adds that one strategy can improve a retiree's odds of never running out of money.

Try to reduce what is for most people their biggest or close to biggest cost over the course of a lifetime: "Take action to reduce your taxes," he says.

Lange emphasizes the buildup and protection of qualified assets through accessing these accounts as late as possible. Then he argues that most retirees should only take minimum required distribution.

"Reducing your taxes will dramatically increase your chances of financial success," Lange writes. "The U.S. tax structure rewards certain actions and punishes others. The difference can mean, literally, millions of dollars."

The issue, Lange says, is by delaying the payment of taxes, "you are giving your accounts more time to add capital gains, interest and dividends, instead of interrupting the buildup of the account."

Hughes says this delayed qualified asset withdrawal strategy is so important that he uses it to the fullest extent.

"Delay taking required minimum distributions from qualified accounts each year until the end of the tax year in December," Hughes says.

Why?

This ensures that you get a few more months of compounding every year. He adds if you are contributing to a qualified plan do the reverse. Try to make all your contributions early in the year so you increase the period of compounding.

Do You Want or Do You Not Want $2 Million?

Lange cites an example of the effect of using and not using the stall the taxman strategy. Two people start out in their 30s both putting $5,000 a year aside for retirement. "Mr. Pay Taxes Later Does Much Better" than "Mr. Pay Taxes Now."

One puts the money into a tax deferred account and the other doesn't. He pays taxes on his investment every year and doesn't use a qualified plan. Both get the same rate of return, about seven percent, but what a difference.

Because he deferred paying taxes on his retirement account and because in retirement he took minimum distributions, "Mr. Pay Taxes Later" got the most from his retirement accounts.

He was the one who followed a policy of protecting qualified assets. He saved a bundle in taxes over the course of a lifetime. "Mr. Pay Taxes Later" will not run out of money, Lange says in reviewing this example.

"Given reasonable assumptions all things being equal, following the adage don't pay taxes now—pay taxes later can be worth almost $2 million over a lifetime," according to Lange.

Some of this scenario of running out of money, of losing that $2 million, is also the result of some people accessing their qualified money too soon, or of retiring too early.

Those retiring in their early 60s, who start taking money out of qualified accounts before they have to or need to, could be taking a risky step, Schwartz, the White Plains, New York advisor, says. It doesn't mean that one must keep working in one's early 60s. It means leaving the qualified assets alone to continue to compound.

Most advisors, although they sometimes hedge on the paying taxes later principle for estate planning reasons, agree with the Lange thesis of paying taxes as late as possible. You ought to go over your strategy with an advisor.

The best strategy, adds Brian Behl, an advisor in Waukesha, Wisconsin, depends on each person's tax situation. But he adds "for many people the best strategy is to spend taxable accounts first, then tax deferred accounts (like 401ks and IRAs), and lastly tax-free accounts like Roth IRAs," he says.

However, because each retirement is unique, Behl emphasizes. There are exceptions to the spend qualified assets last scenario. Say someone is in a low tax bracket in his or her 60s, but will be in a higher tax bracket after taking Social Security and required distributions from qualified accounts.

"If that is the case," he adds, "it can be beneficial to pull income forward through IRA distributions or Roth conversions to maximize lower tax brackets now at a lower rate than is assumed to be paid later."

Still, delaying the use of qualified money could be the most important step in making a retirement plan work, he says.

"That can mean an enormous increase in your retirement savings," Schwartz says. He cautions that those retiring too early, who start taking money from qualified accounts from in their early 60s, could "be doing irreversible damage to the portfolio," he warns.

What damage?

One is interrupting the compounding effect, he adds. That is the ability of money to create money as a portfolio grows, which is the source of wealth. And continuing to grow one's portfolio can be important even for people in their 60s.

Many of us are in better health than our parents and grand-parents. Some will live into their 90s. Think about that in drawing up a retirement plan. It is easy to make mistakes with these assets it took you decades to accumulate. Indeed, I've seen some of the mistakes. They weren't pretty. Here's one.

Chapter 17

The Wrong Way to Use Qualified Assets

How I Saw a Friend Throw Away Her Retirement Assets

Don't make this mistake. Don't let a friend make this mistake. Don't let a child or a grandchild make this mistake.

Please.

Here's a great way to ruin one's retirement plan. You do it by wrecking the principle of compounding, which we have seen is a big factor in creating wealth.

Yet interrupting the compounding factor is what millions of consumer crazy people do every time they pass by a showroom or hear that there is a one-time sale and they must buy now.

Do what I am about to recount and you ensure that you will miss the chance to accumulate significant retirement money. I saw the mistake. I am sick thinking about it decades later.

Working at a financial publication years ago, a young woman I knew at another business publication in the same company—who was a financial journalist and should have known better—decided to break into her qualified retirement account so she could buy a car. She lived in Manhattan and didn't need a car. I suppose it was nice to have a car—and expensive as anything to keep it up—but it was anything but a necessity. She would still have her job without the car.

She had about $30,000 in her qualified retirement account. However, since she was using the account before age 59.5 and since there were no exceptional circumstances, such as a medical event, the government penalized her 10 percent for breaking into her account early. It also required she pay all the investment taxes before she received what was left of her qualified account, which was reduced by the taxes and penalties.

A Really Expensive Car

I hope she enjoyed her car—which she barely had enough money to buy—because it came at quite a price: Now her retirement account was wiped out. But she had her set of wheels. Not only was the account lost, along with employer matching contributions and tax breaks, so were years of compounding. I know many people like cars and I admit I'm the opposite, but was it worth it?

Advisors tell clients that, at any age, and regardless of whether you are trying to build or preserve assets, understand how important the compounding process is in building or preserving wealth. It is the key factor in determining if many people will be able to live comfortably into their 60s and beyond.

At a retirement plan sponsor conference I attended decades ago, a plan official pleaded with employers to help their employees understand how important it was to contribute on a consistent basis to qualified accounts and to not break into them before retirement unless there was a personal emergency.

"For many of your employees," he warned, "this will be their only chance to accumulate significant assets."

Why did he say that?

Many Americans tend to have little in savings outside of their qualified accounts. Many surveys have shown that tens of millions of Americans have less than $1,000 in savings and they're not all poor people with low-income jobs. A lot of them have good middle-class incomes, yet their finances are so bad that a sudden $5,000 bill hurls them into financial disaster. They ending up borrowing thousands of dollars, paying 20 percent interest. They are on the road to financial serfdom, a road built and maintained by credit card companies.

Yet many of them, like my friend, make middle class incomes and have promising careers ahead of them (My friend had a much more successful career than I ever did. She went on to work for a major wire service).

We see these kinds of anti-saving prejudices all around us, in the actions of friends, neighbors and colleagues; in the framing of anti-capital tax codes.

We have developed a prejudice against savings and it shows up in mainstream media. A CBS Radio Network News business reporter, Jill Schlesinger, recently was asked about how people would use another proposed $1,200 stimulus check and its effect on the economy. She dismissed it with the disparaging comment, "They'd probably just save it."

What?

It sounded as though that would be the worst thing for the economy and for millions of individuals.

But that is what millions of Americans need to do! And the fastest growing economies in the world tend to be those with the highest savings rates. So I disagree with her comment.

Part of the problem is the mentality of the welfare state. Many Americans, the same as many citizens in other advanced welfare states, think the government will take care of them.

Please, for your own good, for the good of your family, don't think that way. The government itself is already running up huge debts. Someday soon, it may be forced to cut back, regardless of whether it is a right wing or left-wing government, on something such as Social Security payments. We'll discuss that soon.

Indeed, I wouldn't depend on the government—any government—to take care of me and my family. That's not being cynical; that's being realistic. In the United States, many elderly people, and people looking ahead to retirement, think Social Security will take care of them. That's a mistake.

Let us examine this in our next chapter.

Chapter 18

Don't Overrely on Social Security

"They ought to call it Social Insecurity."

Dorcas Hardy, former Social Security Commissioner, from her book on Social Security

Social Security shouldn't be your primary retirement income.

Social Security doesn't provide adequate retirement income, numerous critics contend.

As the primary retirement savings tool and biggest tax for millions of Americans, it is a bad deal.

There are at least two reasons to debate the merits of Social Security: One, most taxpayers, if they conservatively invested their Social Security payments in a diversified portfolio of stocks and bonds, would get a much better return than what they are projected to receive in Social Security payments.

Second, the Social Security Trust Fund is in bad shape. Various governments, both left and right, have "borrowed" from the fund to make their deficits seem less bad. This, combined with fewer workers paying in and more retirees living longer and collecting more, have led to trust fund deficits.

What's Wrong with Social Security

Over the last few years, the system has run in the red—more

money going out of the system than money going in—and the reserves of the system have been running down. A recent Social Security Trustees report is reporting some troubling numbers.

Indeed, in a recent Social Security's annual Trustees Report showed Social Security ran a gigantic $9 trillion deficit between 2019 and 2020.

The system's long-term unfunded liability is some . That's up from the previous year. These Social Security deficits don't seem to draw comment from our lawmakers, who I believe think they can just continue to pass the problem to the next generation. I believe this it is a reflection of their mismanagement of the system.

The press also tends to ignore these deficits because it is not part of the "official" federal debt. Yet this red ink is real. I believe it will mean changes in the program: Benefits will likely be cut at some point and taxes raised. Why do I say this? It is because this is the way previous Social Security crises have been handled.

Something, says an economist who has followed the problems of the Social Security system, must be done about these deficits. Economist Laurence Kotlikoff, also says that government leaders, including the trustees responsible for ensuring the soundness of the program, are ignoring Social Security's increasing red ink.

"The unfunded liability is the most important and scariest number in the report. The secretary and his fellow trustees ignored it in their summary statement for the same reason they buried it at the rear end of their report. It's political dynamite," according to Kotlikoff.

Social Security Is a Terrible 'Investment' - Intellectual Takeout

Don't Depend on It

What these troubling numbers mean, many advisors say, is that Social Security shouldn't be a big part of your retirement income; not 50 percent or more. 25 percent or less would be a better number.

Why?

Many critics argue mandatory Social Security is a poor investment. It only provides an average annual income of some $18,000 or so. They complain this is a lousy return based on what the average person pays in over the course of a lifetime. I remember in my 20s and 30s, when I had a low salary, the Social Security tax was my biggest tax payment. I believe that most people would obtain a better return if their Social Security money went into private investments.

"Americans would be better off keeping their payroll tax contributions and putting them into private retirement accounts than having to sacrifice them to the government's broken Social Security system," according to the Heritage Foundation's study "Is Social Security Worth Its Cost?"

Social Security officials defend the program as more than just retirement income. They say it provides disability and other benefits not offered in the private sector (Please see the next chapter: "Still a Good Deal, Social Security Official Says").

Social Security, collected through payroll taxes, is the biggest tax many younger and low/middle income workers' pay. Critics contend younger workers, with decades to invest, miss the opportunity to amass significant assets because of high payroll taxes.

Social Security's revenues are collected through payroll taxes levied at 6.2 percent each on the worker and the employer.

This doesn't include an additional 1.45 percent for Medicare, a separate payroll deduction paid by both the worker and the employer. The worker pays the entire bill if an independent contractor.

There is no opt out on this tax. You pay these taxes from the day you start working whether you want to or not; whether you think a private retirement system would be better or not. You're stuck, whether you like the system or not. No one ever asks you what you think of the system or if you would like some of your Social Security "contributions" put into some private investment. So, what do you get after decades of mandatory payments into this system?

The average Social Security recipient receives about $1,600 a month, although most seniors now pay a tax on these payments. These payments were untaxed until the 1980s. That's when, because the system was in trouble owing to mismanagement by both left wing and right-wing governments, new "revenues sources" (taxes) had to be added. Why? The system, despite frequent tax hikes, was running the red.

Some Will Be Forced to Lose Money

The Heritage Foundation study found younger workers paying into Social Security over decades will lose the most. Their returns on their taxes will be between minus -0.04 percent and minus -14.53!

What kind of retirement "investment" is this? You are losing money on one of your big retirement savings vehicles. That is bad when you consider that this is a program that most American workers and their employers must fund.

"We are telling young people to put money into this program that guarantees zero or negative returns," says Rachel Greszler, one of the report's authors.

Greszler notes this is versus a 4.76 percent annual return for those conservatively invested: half in stocks and half in government bonds, according to the study.

However, at my prompting, Greszler conceded the long-term results of diversified private investments are likely better than 4.76 percent since the long-term return of stocks is about 9.5 percent and bonds net between about two and five percent. That's depending on the riskiness of the bond and its duration.

"We wanted to do a conservative study," Greszler says.

Nevertheless, even this conservative projection is much better than what the average retiree will receive in Social Security.

The Social Security Debate Continues

Social Security taxes and benefits have been much debated. Taxes have been raised and benefits cut many times over several generations of Social Security politics, which often results in higher taxes on workers and not facing up to the long-term problems of the systems. They have been caused in part by demographics, politics and generations of mismanagement.

Social Security's trustees, in previous reports, say its trust funds are in the red.

The Trustees projected that "the combined trust funds will be depleted in 2035." That means, if current trends continue, average payments will have to be cut.

Why?

The current system is paying out more in benefits than it is receiving in taxes. It is running into problems for at least two reasons:1) Fewer workers are paying into the system than a decade or two ago as the birthrate is slowing. By the way, here is an argument for allowing increased numbers of legal, not illegal, immigrants who would pay these payroll taxes.

2)Governments of the past few generations, when the system was running in black owing to higher taxes and strong economic growth, tended to "borrow" (arrogate?) money from the system. They, both Republican and Democratic governments, used surpluses for anything they wanted or to make deficits seem smaller. This violated the principle of the system, which is supposed to be based on a trust fund; that funds going into this system must be dedicated to one thing: paying for it, not paying for whatever government program some pol wants.

So, once again the system is facing problems. I say once again because periodic crises have affected the program several times since it began in 1935. They usually mean recipients get less and those people paying into the system pay more.

Hence, many advisors specializing in retirement planning caution clients not to over rely on Social Security.

"I tell people to be very conservative about Social Security payments in building a retirement plan," says Ronald Roge, a Bohemia, New York advisor. "It should be no more than a third of your income."

Charles Hughes, a longtime advisor in Bay Shore, New York who writes a lot of retirement plans, warns that "if a client is expecting to get most of his income from Social Security, then there is very little I can do to help." Hughes contends that Social Security should be less than 50 percent of anyone's retirement income.

Beside the individual effects of Social Security, there are also macro implications to a nation dependent on Social Security, according to critics.

Supporters of privatizing some part of Social Security contend it would do more to help millions save more for retirement. They say that reforms would also have macro-economic benefits that could be felt throughout the economy.

Besides helping millions of individuals trying to save enough for retirement, reforms would also make our economy more productive.

Former presidential advisor Martin Feldstein said each dollar put into Social Security by a worker or an employer reduces private saving by 87 cents. He argued allowing some or all of Social Security contributions to go into private investments would improve national savings rates.

This would expand the nation's capital pool. More capital would lower the price of money. The latter is otherwise known as interest rates.

Tens of millions of us are affected by every change in interest rates. Even a small drop in interest means some of them can get a mortgage and a home. The opposite locks them out of the housing market.

Greszler complains high Social Security taxes foster "income inequality." Those with low incomes, she says, "have less to invest than those with higher incomes."

She warns Social Security, with a deficit of some $16 trillion, will have a payment cut of some 20 percent if changes aren't made by 2035. Private account options are critical for young people.

However, Greszler predicts private Social Security retirement accounts will not be will offered in the short term by either Republicans or Democrats. This is logical since both Republican and Democratic administrations have made this mess. It would be embarrassing to many of them to clean it up. So what will happen in the next crisis?

She fears the conventional solutions will be used to save the system: Payroll taxes will be raised and benefits cut. Nevertheless, Social Security has many defenders. Let's talk to one.

Chapter 19

A Q&A with Social Security's Chief Actuary Stephen Goss

Social Security is more comprehensive than the private retirement account proposed by critics. That's what a Social Security official told me a few years ago in response to the Heritage Foundation's study arguing that young people will receive a negative return on their Social Security taxes.

"It is important to note that Social Security provides much more than a retirement pension. About one third of benefits paid are for disability and survivors insurance protection," said Stephen Goss, Social Security's Chief Actuary. "Such benefits cannot be provided from individual savings in a retirement account."

Goss also asserts that some people wouldn't do well in private retirement accounts in part because private sector firms would charge high management fees.

"It is important," Goss says in an interview I did for a story in the New York Post years ago, "to consider administrative costs for the accumulation and distribution periods of any benefit program. Personal accounts invested in private markets can incur administrative costs of one percent or more a year."

(By the way, I believe that Goss' number is right about a lot of mutual funds. However, this is not true for well-run index funds as we have detailed in a previous chapter).

These administrative costs could reduce the private accounts accumulation by 70 percent, he adds. Goss said Social Security administrative costs are less.

A System in Crisis

However, both critics and defenders of Social Security can agree on this: The system faces a crisis in the near future. Some were saying this even before the recent Coronavirus disaster started increasing the pace of government deficits and debt. Goss says that the program's "reserves will become depleted in 2035."

If the deficits aren't closed, that would mean a 20 percent cut in benefits, Goss says. He adds, in a sentiment that the program's critics echo, that "Congress will need to act." He expects that it will. This is not the first time the system has faced problems.

Is Social Security a bad deal as many critics claim? Is the system rally in trouble. A few years ago I spoke with Goss about that and other Social Security issues

GB: Wouldn't people get a better deal if their Social Security taxes were privately invested in a portfolio of stocks and bonds?

SG: It is important to note that Social Security provides much more than just a retirement pension. About one third of benefits paid are for disability and survivors insurance protection. Such benefits cannot be provided from individual savings in a retirement account.

GB: But what about the investment returns of Social Security? They're not very good; in fact, in some cases their long-term returns are now projected to be negative.

SG: Social Security Trust Fund reserves must be invested in interest bearing securities backed by the full faith and credit of the U.S. government. Some have proposed allowing the trust fund reserves to be invested at least partly in private securities (stocks and bonds), which would be more volatile but would provide a higher expected rate of return. One such proposal was put forth by Senators Kerrey and Simpson years ago. . In addition, it is important to consider administrative costs for the accumulation and distribution periods of any benefit program.

GB: You're saying that personal accounts aren't a good deal for the average retiree?

SG: Personal accounts invested in private markets can incur administrative costs of 1 percent or more per year, so that the portion of the accumulation actually paid in benefits may be 70 percent or less. The portion can be even less for private disability ad life insurance. For Social Security, administrative costs are less than 1 percent on a lifetime basis.

GB: Yet the Heritage Foundation writes that older workers are getting a very low rate of return on their Social Security and that younger workers will actually see returns of negative 14 percent versus just under five percent in a basket of stocks and bonds invested 50/50. How can anyone justify poor Social Security returns versus private investment conservatively invested over the long term.

SG: Rates of return on Social Security are complicated because these benefits include disability and survivors protection as well as CPI-indexed life annuities for retirees, something not offered in the commercial market. The value of such insurance protection goes beyond just the average benefit payments, as indicated by the premiums charged for commercial insurance protection. Note that the accumulation in personal savings accounts can vary widely based on timing and investment choices. As a result, serious proposals for providing some portion of Social Security protection in the form of individual accounts have generally provided some form of guaranteed return to eliminate the prospect that some individuals will have poor experience.

GB: And what would that be?

SG: An example is the "Social Security Personal Savings and Prosperity Act" introduced by Paul Ryan, which evolved over several years providing successive versions of individual protection.
https://www.ssa.gov/OACT/solvency/PRyan_20080521.pdf
https://www.ssa.gov/OACT/solvency/RyanSununu_20050420.pdf
https://www.ssa.gov/OACT/solvency/PRyan_20040719.pdf

For a more comprehensive look at the returns provided to individuals from Social Security, see annual analyses on internal rates of return at https://www.ssa.gov/oact/NOTES/ran5/index.htmland annual analyses of returns relative to treasury yields (money's worth ratios) at https://www.ssa.gov/oact/NOTES/ran7/index.html. But again, remember that these analyses do not include the value of risk pooling provided in insurance and annuities.

GB: Nevertheless, many studies show various groups with shorter lifespans get little or sometimes nothing from Social Security. How can one defend that?

SG: Regarding individuals with lower life expectancies, note that such individuals tend to have higher disability incidence, and of course tend to provide more benefits to survivors. At this point the analyses indicated above do not reflect the differential risk of disability and so underestimate the value of Social Security for lower paid individuals who also tend to have higher mortality and disability rates.

GB: Let's go back to the issue of savings. Martin Feldstein, an advisor to President Reagan, argued that privatizing some or all of Social Security would help national savings rates, would improve the capital stock and lower the price of money, otherwise known as interest rates. Was he wrong?

SG: Regarding contribution to national investment and capital stock, we should consider what the effects would be if Social Security had been set up as a fully advance funded program, rather than as a "pay as you go" current cost financed program, maintaining only small reserves as a "contingency reserve" to allow the Congress time to act if conditions are for a period worse than anticipated for Social Security financing. If full advance funding had been specified, then Social Security payroll taxes for those entering employment would have been several times the initial level in 1937, and retirement benefits would not have been paid for many decades later, rather than in 1940. Because payroll taxes were initially low, this allowed workers to invest directly in private markets, contributing to the expansive capital stock we have in the U.S. today.

GB: So part of the problem over the past 30 years or so is that reserves have been spent on other things?

SG: Had Social Security maintained reserves to fully advance fund future benefit obligations, the trust funds would now hold well in excess of $20 trillion in assets, with the government controlling these investments rather than the public.

A further consideration for the prospect of providing personal accounts in lieu of a portion of Social Security retirement benefits was explored in detail by the President's Commission to Strengthen Social Security. A major consideration is that in transforming Social Security from a largely pay as you go financed program to one with advance funding, there is a substantial transition cost, or "transition investment" needed over several years where past benefit obligations still need to be met from taxes on current workers, while these same workers would also be contributing to their own personal accounts. As seen in the memorandum to the chairs of the commission these costs are substantial.

GB: Economist Lester Thurow once said of social insurance programs in general: The first generation does great. The second generation does not do as well. By the third generation, they are scrambling to pay for the system. It sounds as though we're in the third generation. Does this mean that Social Security taxes will have to be raised again?

SG: As indicated above, Social Security reserves are intended to provide contingency reserves to allow Congress time to react if events, like a major recession, temporarily make the current law pay as you go financing inadequate. Such circumstances have arisen many times in the history of the program and Congress has always responded in a timely fashion to ensure continued payment of benefits scheduled in the law. In the latest Trustees Report of 2019 we project that combined OASI and DI Trust Fund reserves will begin to decline in 2020 as they are used to augment current payroll tax contributions for the full and timely payment of benefits. Under the intermediate projections, we estimate that the reserves will become depleted in 2035 in the absence of any Congressional action, at which point continuing payroll tax contributions would still be sufficient to cover 80 percent of scheduled benefits. Thus, Social Security will not "run out of money."

GB: Yet funding is now a problem

SG: Between now and 2035 the Congress will need to act, either raising the amount of revenue scheduled in the law, or lowering the level of benefits scheduled in the law, or some combination of these approaches. The history of the program tells us that s has always acted timely to assure that the trust fund reserves will not become depleted. We should be confident that the Congress will continue in this fashion in the future.

GB: Thanks, Mr. Goss

Chapter 20

Another Reason Why You Always Need Some Cash in Your Portfolio

What appears to be the worst performing asset can sometimes be the best.

In preserving wealth you worked decades to build it is important to play defense sometimes. In difficult times it is vital to have a cash reserve to shield you from having to use investment assets that are compounding. There's always another reason to have some cash. A mutual fund expert once noted an anomaly of the investing world: The worst will sometimes be first. That means often unloved cash, the Rodney Dangerfield "I don't get no respect," of investment categories, is sometimes the best performing asset category. It doesn't happen often and it doesn't go on for very long periods, but once in a while it happens.

Indeed, cash isn't always trash, for short periods when bonds and stocks reek.

Yes, stocks beat cash over the long term and in most short periods. However, there are still periods, even as long as a decade, when cash is a better investment than stocks, according to a Lending Tree.com study. In fact, in a recent 51-year period, cash was the best-performing asset 30 percent of the time, the study found.

I Want Some CDs, Please

Hard times for equities often mean all that glitters is not financial assets but garden-variety cash—in certificates of deposit (CDs).

"Unsurprisingly, CDs outperform stocks more often during economic recessions and underperform during economic expansion, although there are pockets of exceptions," according to the study.

The author of the study said this should remind investors that over-relying on any one asset class is dangerous.

"We did this study as a wake-up call to make people understand that one needs more than just stocks and bonds as a diversifier—that stocks and bonds can sometimes go down together as in 2008," said Brian Karimzad, vice president of research for Magnify Money, a LendingTree subsidiary.

Here's the Case for Cash

He added that, for the average investor, cash can be important for a number of reasons. A cash reserve can be critical in hard times. That's when someone has lost a job for instance, something that millions of Americans are grappling with today.

Cash can also be an effective investment when equities are pricey, Karimzad said.

Six-month certificates of deposit, for example, did very well at the beginning of the period known as the "lost decade," the study said. That's when CDs had the longest time of beating stocks, a 33-month period from 2000 to 2003.

"The one-year return of six-month CDs beat the one-year return of stocks for 33 consecutive months," according to the study.

In the 1970s and 2000s, the study noted, there were periods when annualized CD performance beat stocks.

Do You Still Have Some Ammo?

Anthony Ogorek, a longtime advisor in Buffalo, New York, says it's good to have some cash for another reason.

"You always want to have some bullets on hand for bad times; to take advantage of unique opportunities to invest." In the midst of a bear market, when good stocks often go on sale because many people are too spooked or cash poor to invest, cash can be very valuable. You have cash, you can harvest great companies but this time at bargain prices.

In the early 1970s, there was an 18-month period when the stock market was terrible, a terrible place that had a lot of bargains. It went down some 40 percent. "I never wanted to come to work," a veteran stock broker told me who lived though that period.

At that time, Warren Buffett had been sitting on the sidelines waiting for the stock market to blow up, with lots of cash, ready to pounce. He bought millions of shares in many of the biggest companies. In some of them, his stake became so big that he was given a seat on the board.

So always have some cash ready to protect yourself or to jump on great investment. There's nothing trashy about opportunity or investment or just being ready for the next disaster on Wall Street.

Chapter 21

Reading Financial Classics, Important for Anyone, Anytime

Some books can make a big difference in achieving financial independence. You don't have to read them all but you can find inspiration from the experience of others. Here are a few.

There is Thomas Stanley's "The Millionaire Next Door." The book could also have been entitled "The World Is Not What You Think It Is."

Stanley, who recently died after running an institute that examined how wealth originated, documented that there is a common money delusion. Some people with the outward signs of wealth aren't rich. Yes, they drive big cars and live in big houses. However, many of them are in hock up to their eyeballs and have little in assets.

By contrast, other people, the ones who seem to have modest lifestyles, are actually wealthy. But they're not interested in showing off. They're content just to have financial independence, and not show off .

They live without calling attention to their wealth. The extreme case of this is Warren Buffett. He doesn't live in the lap of luxury. That's despite many offers to come to New York and run various investment businesses. Instead, he lives in the same house in Omaha, Nebraska that he has had for generations. He bought it for a small price.

What is the common characteristic of Stanley's next store millionaires? They all under consume. They not only under consume, but when they consume they are all looking for discounts. Even in wealthy, not overspending is in their DNA.

Looking for Discounts Everywhere

However, looking for discounts shouldn't be limited to shopping. Looking and finding discounts is a very important factor in achieving financial independence. And that's why reading the books of the founder of the Vanguard mutual fund family can be so important. John Bogle's "Commonsense on Mutual Funds" is the best known. It is a great book by a fund leader who thought very seriously about how the often taken for granted average individual investor could do well by avoiding the costly traps set by much of Wall Street.

But all Bogle's books are valuable. They stress the same theme of this book—don't waste money. It is in not wasting money, in taking advantage of every opportunity, that you, a middle-class person, achieve financial independence.

Bogle was a money maverick who made a lot of average people wealthier, thanks to his funds. Many people who used his ideas were able to provide a much better standard of living for themselves and their loved ones.

Bogle was a man who turned the mutual fund industry upside down with the revolutionary idea of passive investing. His idea was not to try to pick certain stocks, but passively and cheaply, invest in an index.

Johnny Bogle Was a Rebel...

His funds didn't try to get huge returns, just good ones at the lowest possible price. He was just trying to hit consistent singles and doubles. He wasn't trying for home runs, which meant trying, and often failing, to get incredible returns every year. Going for homers, trying to get twenty percent a year or more every year, means you also strike out a lot; you also lose 20 percent some years.

A go for broke approach often gets lousy returns for the investor, Bogle believed. By contrast, consistently obtaining good returns at a lower price, he said, is an approach that is ideal for the average investor. This approach maximizes compounding.

That, he believed, was much better than what was offered by most funds when he started his then pipsqueak Vanguard fund company in the 1970s with a few million dollars. A half century of so later, Vanguard became one of the biggest fund complexes. Vanguard also has an unusual corporate structure. It has trillions of dollars in individual assets. The assets belong to the investors, not to the investment company. It is this unusual legal structure that tends to protect investors. The investors benefit from the unusual way the funds are dispersed; not directly in stocks but through indexes representing baskets of stocks.

Yet John Bogle didn't invent index investing, a concept that he studied for years before starting his company. Indexing had been used by a few institutional investors in the 1960s and 1970s, but he brought it into the mainstream. His upstart company, the Vanguard Group of Funds, which was much scorned when it began, brought the concept to the masses. By keeping costs low—it took a very small minimum for someone to start a Vanguard account unlike other pricier fund complexes—he found an effective way to bring passive investing to the average small investor. He connected with the small investor, looking for a way to invest for the long term. My wife and I were two of them.

Bogle warned that most funds, and most of the securities industry, were flawed; that they were biased in favor of institutions; biased against the individual investor.

D'accord!

The industry then and now often sell outrageously expensive products. Indeed, some fund companies spend money like the average candidate for Congress in an election year.

Caring About the Individual

Today the success of his company seems undisputed. Yet, in the beginning, it was a struggle for Bogle and his allies. For the first few years, there wasn't a lot of Vanguard inflows. The whole indexing concept was ridiculed by many money managers. They had a stake in keeping things as they were because they made a bundle from investment fees, much of which were wiped out by the Bogle model.

In a recent book Bogle detailed the problems he confronted when he started Vanguard. Back in the beginning, the fund industry was a very different place.

For instance, I remember, when I began writing about funds in the late 1980s, most funds came with sales charges; often as high as eight percent.

Think of it. Let's say you invested, or tried to invest, $10,000 in a fund. You had a big haircut coming. Only $9,200 of your money was invested. The rest went into a sales charge. And this was a standard of fund industry at that time! Some standard. It was, I thought, obscene. But there were more hijinks. Banks looked at the trillions of dollars pouring into investment companies and, in effect, said, "why should fund companies have all the fun?"

I remember my bank, J.P. Morgan/Chase, seeing how fund business was exploding in the 1980s, thought it should jump into the fund pool. It got into the act with its own line of overpriced funds with lots of sales charges and egregious expense ratios. How was the performance?

Lousy.

On top of that most actively managed funds carried high expense ratios; maybe one or one and a half percent higher than Vanguard funds.

Why was Vanguard better then and now?

They did little trading and charged a pittance compared to the high priced, actively managed, funds. I once interviewed Vanguard's head trader, Gus Sauter, for Traders Magazine. He explained how he used limit orders to ensure that, when Vanguard bought shares, the company got the greatest discounts. His philosophy was so different from much of the spend big securities industry. Funds, he said, should be cheaper and cheaper still as the industry accumulates more and more assets. This, I believe, was best thing for his clients. It's why Vanguard and similar fund companies have many average people financially independent.

Here's another painful fact: Most of these pricy funds don't beat indexes. And only a small percentage of the funds that do beat indexes, do it on a regular basis. The few winners among active funds often changes from year to year, making it difficult or well-nigh impossible to find the hot manager. That's part of what I learned from reading the sage Bogle.

One reaches an inevitable conclusion: Passive investing in general is a much better deal than active investing for the average investor. The latter was a conclusion reached by Warren Buffett, who has been a big Bogle fan.

Bogle's argument was that low costs are very important over the long run. When one figures in over the other the advantages of avoiding active management expenses—such as passive investing triggers a smaller tax bill than active investing—it is reasonable to say that passive investing, on average, can generate about two percent a year better returns than active investing over the long term. Maybe more, depending on how one is figuring the taxes and the myriad transaction costs.

What does this mean for a person who Bogle was designing his products for, the average Joe? Over the long term it was huge. Let's say he or she invested $300 a month over 40 years. One person gets seven percent on his or her money. That person has some $792,000 after 40 years. The other person, who found a way to get two percent better returns, ends up with $1,414,000.

What a difference!

That is the difference that Bogle provided for millions of investors.

Buffett suggested there should be statute recognizing how Bogle helped the average investor.

I'd guess, if that statute was ever erected, it would be defaced by a Wall Street mob of outraged financial professionals, the types who thought index investing produced mediocre returns.

Many of the latter were people who insisted, in face of evidence to the contrary, that passive investing was "Un-American" or that it was a form of Marxism. The latter criticism is hilarious. It was offered by a big institutional brokerage firm that, unsurprisingly, will not provide me with the original literature in which it compared Bogle to Marx.

My wife and I have used Vanguard funds for decades. They are a big reason why we are financially independent today.

Some Other Books

There are many other books that are worth your time Benjamin Graham's "The Intelligent Investor," the bible of value investing. It gives you a step-by-step approach to finding undervalued stocks and avoiding pricey ones.

"Investing the Templeton Way," is also a wonderful book by his niece, Lauren C. Templeton.

It explains how Templeton went from nothing to billionaire by investing in things that other people shunned, and why, when things are dire, it is the best time to invest.

"The Money Masters by John Train is terrific. It shows how varied investors made their fortunes.

Besides interviewing many brilliant, and not so brilliant, investors, Train, a successful investment advisor, provides some commonsense rules. Here are a few of them.

One, only buy a stock as a share in a good business that you know a lot about.

Second, buy when stocks have few friends—particularly the stock in question.

Third, Be patient. Don't be rattled by fluctuations.

Fourth, Invest, don't guess.

Both Templeton and Buffett rate very good chapters in Train's book. Templeton's greatness didn't come from looking for good times, but the worst of times. He wanted cheapness and bad times so he could buy a boatload of shares of a targeted company or market.

"To summarize," Lauren Templeton writes of her uncle, "bargain hunters seek volatility in stock prices to find opportunities and panicked selling creates the most volatility, usually of historically high levels. Bargain hunters seek misconception, and panic at the height of the overwhelming presence of fear."

Understanding that fear, understanding the basic greed and fear of human beings, is part of what made Templeton a great investor. That and a sense of modesty.

In the late 1990s, Buffett and Templeton couldn't understand these pricey new technology companies. So they stayed away from them and were said by some myopic observers to be over the hill.

Yet they were brilliant because, unlike many other more celebrated investors, they missed the crash of 2001. Indeed, Templeton shorted a lot of the Internet investments and made a bundle. By the way, many people don't like short sellers—or investors who warn that something is overpriced—but it was the short sellers more than the regulators who exposed how overpriced Enron stock was.

Reading quality investment books can help one recognize the investment frauds. There's still lots of them around today. They'd like to get a big piece of your investment pie. Be careful, Mr. and Mrs. Investor. Many in the investment world would like to get your money and give you very little.

Chapter 22

Do You Need an Advisor? How to Find One

But is he or she worth the fees?

Finding a good advisor is the anomaly of the financial services industry. The problem is, if one is starting out and needs an advisor because one has little or no assets and just has a middle-class income, it's difficult to find one. Many advisors don't believe they can make money from you because today you have few or no assets. Their bosses want them to bring in million-dollar accounts.

On the other hand, if you have much less of a need for an advisor because you already have a lot of assets and a high income, then advisors will find you. You sometimes don't need them, but they will offer you wonderful deals.

This is the contradiction of the money management/advisor business. The people who need the service the most often can't get it. Those who need it the least, have lots of good choices.

(By the way, before you curse the bosses of these big brokerages, remember many of these firms have such large overhead costs that they only have profitable relationships with those who have considerable assets. However, the comeback on this is one should develop relationships with young investors who, although they don't have a ton of money today, have the potential to develop six or seven figure accounts a decade or two down the road).

I recently experienced this strange problem of whether or not some big financial institution wants your business. My wife and I sold our own second apartment, our investment apartment. After the closing, we deposited three good size checks in our J.P. Morgan/Chase "high interest" (sic) money market account. It has a small interest rate. So we don't keep a lot of our assets with the bank. The low rates are true with most banks, institutions that often take their retail/individual, customers for granted and goes into seventh heaven at the thought of new institutional business.

I only did so to get rid on the money for a day or so because I didn't want to carry around the checks in a bad part of New York City. Two days later, this money was moved to a Vanguard money market account. It was paying a more reasonable interest rate. Before I did, I received an unexpected call from my bank.

I have been a J.P. Morgan/Chase customer for decades. It is a matter of convenience. There are Chase branches all over although their ATMs these days seem to break down more frequently than before. So, we usually keep a small percentage of our assets with them, maybe $10,000 or less. I had rarely, if ever, heard from them over decades. Now, since my account had a lot more cash, J.P. Morgan Chase bankers now became our new best friends.

Indeed, with hundreds of thousands of dollars parked in one of their accounts, I was suddenly a somebody. I got several calls from people from Chase. But, in the all the previous years, I have conducted business with them—credit cards, a checking and saving account as well as we finished the last few years of our mortgage with them when our previous mortgage bankers went out of business—they looked at me as a nobody. Now they loved me.

All those years when they might have helped me, they were nowhere to be found. Now it was different. Now they seemed to realize that they we had substantial assets.

So the people who could use the help of big financial institutions the most, can't get them or get lousy services. I wasn't surprised. It's tough to find experienced financial professionals to work with the average individual investor, whether we are talking about banks or brokerages.

It has been my business for a good part of my life to write about the services offered by various financial professionals, such as certified financial planners (CFPs), Certified Public Accountants (CPA), Registered Investment Advisors (RIAs) and brokers, often known as RRs (registered representatives), among others. How does one find good financial professionals?

Organizations such as the Financial Planning Association (FPA) and the National Association of Personal Financial Advisors (NAPFA) will have lists of approved professionals. Try them. They will send you a list of people in your area.

At the end of this chapter, I will name a few of the professionals I have interviewed over the years who I believe are worth your time. In every case, I have no professional relationship with any of these people other than I have interviewed them for various publications such as Financial Advisor, Financial Planning or The New York Post business section, among others.

In finding an advisor here are certain principles that should cover anyone you hire.

Be sure the professional is a fiduciary

This is simply the principle that the professional puts the interests of the client before that of his or her employer. It may seem a logical assumption. However, don't take it for granted. More and more of the financial services industry is moving toward this standard, but be sure the profession-al is always working in your interest. Examine his or her credentials. There are still some people who bill themselves as advisors who don't have any significant credentials. For example, I think a person who is a CFP, a certified financial planner, or a CPA, a certified public accountant, has a serious commitment to the financial services business. Someone who just has a license to sell securities may not.

Ask How He or She Is Paid

It's important how much the professional is paid. Remember we have discussed how important it is to keep costs low if you expect to reach a goal. Is the professional a fee only or fee and commission or commission only?

These are important issues that are vital to the quality of service you will receive. Commissions are paid to some pro-fessionals every time a financial product is sold. That can motivate some financial professionals to get the client to buy more financial products than necessary or to buy the wrong ones. Some financial professionals, for example, are never going to recommend that you buy low-cost products such as index funds. That's because these products don't generate a lot in commissions, which some advisors love, even though they are often the best products for many clients.

Fee based compensation is better. It is based on how much the client has in an account. As the account grows in value, the value of the fee grows. Some professionals collect their income through of a mix of fee and commission-based busi-ness.

In general, this increasing the client's wealth incentive is often the best way of paying the financial professional; of keeping the client's and the advisor's interests on the same page.

For instance, one percent of a $1 million account is twice as profitable to a financial professional as one percent of a $500,000 account. He or she makes more when the value of your account goes up as opposed to the being paid a commission every time a financial product is sold.

Fee based work is a much more sensible approach to compensating the professional and keeping the professional's interests aligned with the client's.

Ask for Referrals and Then Some

Don't just ask the potential advisor for referrals, also ask your friends and neighbors who have advisors. Ask how have their advisors worked out?

Will you feel comfortable with this person? What is she or he like? Does the professional have a regular schedule of updating your situation? Is he or she proactive in a time of crisis? For instance, the Covid crisis caused problems with markets. Did your advisor call to check up and update your situation? If your advisor doesn't call you in crisis situations, then you should consider another.

Have a Sample Session with a Potential Advisor

Let an advisor provide you with a free sample session. Are you comfortable with the professional?

Sometimes a professional is qualified but you just don't connect. Don't be afraid to look elsewhere. In a strong financial relationship, it is almost as if you are getting married. In advisory services or in going to the altar be sure this is the right one.

Check his or her record. Does this professional have a clean record? Check his or her ADV record, which tracks an advisor's disciplinary history, among other things. The advisor should be able, and happy to supply these records and, if not, there is something wrong.

Over years of business reporting for various publications, I have come across various professionals who I believe are outstanding. Their base of knowledge is considerable. They have many years of experience. I have always found these professionals to be consumer friendly.

Here are just a few of them. One of these advisers might be right for you, but it all depends on what you need or what. One other note: No one is paying me a centavo to recommend them. I have not gone over with them what I am about to say. These are my impressions based on years of dealing with them.

*Charles Hughes, CFP, Bayshore, New York, cghughes@cgh ughesco.com. is one of the founders of the financial planning movement. This was a movement that has brought credibility to the little known certified financial planner designation (CFP).

The designation, CFP, certified financial planner, now has become a professional standing of great distinction. That is in part thanks to the efforts of Hughes over more than 30 years. He is a man of high standards. If I weren't a reporter, a reporter who had dealt with Hughes many times, and was looking for an adviser, he would be the kind of person I would want helping me manage my money and helping me achieve goals such as a secure retirement. The latter is his specialty.

*Bernard M. Kiely, Bernie@Kiely.com, CPA, CFP, Morristown, New Jersey is an outstanding professional. Again, I have known Kiely for decades. He is a person of great knowledge and has built his business into one of the better advisory services around. He offers free talks, trying to educate people in the basics of financial planning and money management. He has a talk on credit cards that is outstanding. Much is reflected in these pages.

*Anthony J. Ogorek (Prosper@Ogorek.com), CFP, Buffalo, New York

Again, I have known him for decades and he has provided commonsense advice for my readers on all kinds of money issues. He is very interested in debt and worried that many young people getting into debt before they even begin their work lives. He thinks some universities are misleading young people about student loans. Like the others mentioned, he is a person of integrity.

I have only noted a few professionals here owing to space limitations. But, in my decades of writing about financial products, there are dozens, perhaps hundreds, of smart, capable people I could mention here. A key issue for me is knowing that, whichever professional you are considering, that you ensure the person has a credential that qualifies him or her. Marks such as the CFP, certified financial planner, or a CPA, certified public accountant, mean that a professional is more than someone who is selling products or is an employee of a big brokerage.

Professional marks mean that a person has gone through an extensive course of training to obtain those designations and has to meet various continuing education requirements throughout his or her professional life to retain them. Anyone with a, say CFP or CPA, doesn't want to lose that designation. The person can lose those marks if he or she acts unethically. These marks are as important to these people as licenses for other professionals to practice law or medicine. The designations are something very important to determining if the person is right for you.

Chapter 23

The Data Breach—Destroying Your Good Work

It's ten p.m., do you know where your assets are?

You've spent decades building up assets and now they could be destroyed. That wealth is often created through part-time jobs or small businesses. The latter is engine of so much new wealth.

However, many of the newly wealthy, people who practice many of the ideas that are preached in this book are facing the potential destruction of their personal and business wealth.

Data Breaches Threaten Everyone's Wealth

Indeed, data breaches not only hurt consumers, but are an expensive nightmare for small businesses, according to a recent study.

"Twenty one percent of (SMBs) small businesses reported a data breach within the last 24 months, up by 17 percent from two years ago. A full 41 percent of small businesses said they were hit by a breach that cost them more than $50,000 to recover," according to a recent Bank of America Merchant Services Small Business Spotlight.

These continuing breaches could threaten the average small business' survival, the study found. That's because "30 percent of consumers surveyed revealed they would never return to a small business that suffered a breach, up from 20 percent two years ago."

Some 500 U.S. based small business and some 500 consumers who patronize small firms were surveyed about breaches.

Cyber Thieves Move Fast

"The breaches continue to rise because crooks are smart and find unique ways to work the system to their advantage." Says Bill Hardekopf, a credit card industry expert. "When card issuers or payment processors close one loophole, crooks find another. Cyber criminals are smart."

What should one do?

Be vigilant, whether it is an individual or a business account, Hardekopf adds.

He advises consumers to check card statements each month. Thieves often place a small transaction that is ignored, he says. "But if that goes through," Hardekopf adds, "then they put through a much larger transaction."

My Business Will Protect Me?

Don't depend on businesses to protect you. Some of them aren't making your security needs a priority. Some, the same as many career pols both left and right, don't care.

Indeed, Verizon, in a recent study of the effect of data breaches on businesses in general, warned some don't take it seriously.

"Organizations are putting speed and profits before mobile security," according to the Verizon Data Breach Investigations Report.

"And the consequences are not surprising: Almost a third (32%) admitted to having sacrificed mobile security to improve expediency and/or business performance—38% of those said that their organization is at significant risk from mobile threats," the report said.

Indeed, with more people conducting business through mobile devices, criminals are running up big bills, especially in the United States, another report says.

The average cost of a data breach globally is $3.92 million, but in the United States it is more than double that ($8.19 million), according to the IBM Security & Ponemon Institute's "Cost of a Data Breach Report 2019."

Not only are the costs huge, but it is a problem, the IBM reports says, that tends to sneak up. The problem, the report warns, strikes in ways few of us would expect. A big part is cyber thievery can go on for months before someone notices.

Indeed, it takes on average 279 days just to identify a data breach, the report said. The damage is "felt for years after the event."

Think of how this could affect you or your business or both. Years of effort and hard work could be wiped. Visit and revisit your security systems whenever possible because cyber criminals are doing the same; looking for breaches they can exploit.

Now it is time to for you to take some final steps to see how can you take advantage of smart money-making opportunities in a period of turmoil; it is time to consider smart money moves as enter another Trump administration.

Postscript - Investing in the Age of Trump----What Now?

The basic ideas of the clever investor—be a transactor, not a revolver, save and invest on a regular basis, over years to achieve financial independence, take advantage of every tax saving opportunity because taxes, over the course of a lifetime will likely be your biggest course—change little from administration to administration. These guiding ideas apply to almost any administration.

President Trump tends to be investor friendly. The Biden administration, embraced many of the ideas of socialist Senator Bernie Saunders, didn't seem to be so. It seemed more interested in "income equality." That was going to try to pass more tax bills aimed at those who have a fair amount of assets and redistribute them to those without substantial assets. This is the classic debate of all republics. It is a very old argument and was discussed by James Madison in the Federalist Papers.

Remember, despite the expected more friendly attitude of the second Trump administrations, all recent administrations, has been running up huge deficits and likely will continue to do so. That could increase debt, interest and inflation rates. These are disturbing issues.

For investing, that means you should consider some investments that are tied to protecting the ravages of inflation. This can mean some hard assets such as gold and silver. It can also mean bonds that are designed to offset some of the problems of inflation such as TIPs, which are treasury inflation protected bonds. If you buy some of the latter, be sure to use a low-cost product with no sales charges. A bit of non-financial assets, such as gold and real estate, can also be included in your portfolio. But whatever you do, remember: Never invest in things you can't understand or because others around are excited and claim to have made a bundle on it,

But let's assume that, owing to the Trump administration or other factors, you're doing better over the next few years.

You're taking home more money, what should you do with it? Save or invest at least half or most of your additional take home pay. Especially for those who have fallen behind in retirement savings and are saving for other things, take maximum advantage of any breaks you get. Don't assume that any tax breaks will continue. It is amazing how presidents can change in office or how succeeding presidents can reverse tax policies.

For instance, President Ronald Reagan cut taxes in the early 1980s. Then later on some taxes were raised in a compromise deal with Democrats. President Bill Clinton, despite protests from his own party, cut the capital gains rate. This helped the economy and millions of investors who were ready to cash in owing to lower rates. Some were ready to sell assets, paying a lot less in taxes when rates dropped because the tax bill would be a lot smaller. At the same time, with more paying taxes, the federal government actually ran a surplus under Clinton at the end of his two terms. Lower taxes helped everyone.

Unfortunately, some later administrations after Clinton's raised taxes. So, make hay while the sun is shining. That is a rule for investors and for life. Opportunities rarely come around multiple times in a person's life. So when they do, jump on them. Unless you live a very long time, it is unlikely you will see them again.

Remember the principles that we have talked about in previous pages. Let's say you have some extra, possibly unexpected, money. Here's a guaranteed terrific investment for some: Pay off credit card debt immediately. These card rates are already high. What happens to you and your card debt if interest rates keep rising? Avoid that danger now and forever.

Therefore, make the commitment to be a transactor, not a revolver for the rest of your life. Then build up a cash reserve so you are never in danger of falling into credit card hell again if you face a period of unemployment, which most people do in an average work life.

Be ready to move in those multiple areas in which Biden wants to raise taxes.

For example, I have a middle-class friend who bought a second apartment many years ago in his co-op at a dirt-cheap insider price of $13,000. The apartment, which is now worth about $300,000, was occupied for many years and now is free to sell.

However, he has had a big problem: If he sells, he will pay a huge capital gains tax, possibly as much as $50,000 of his gain will go to the government because capital gains rates are now high. After all the risks this man went through over the years of buying as well as holding on to the apartment and experiencing losses, the idea of having to kick back a large part of his gain makes him sick.

What should he do?

He should grimace and pay the big tax bill now. Why? Because it is possible that under a future administration capital gains bill will be a lot higher later.

None of this is guaranteed. There are things you can control in your financial life, which is what this book is all about, and things you can't. The latter is what religion is all about. Some things we can do for ourselves. Some things require prayer.

The U.S. government has been on a spending spree for years. It has run up incredible debts and needs to find new revenues. That's where it continued to go under President Biden. Well, he has already raised taxes on all of us through higher inflation rates. He has also said that he wants to raise the corporate tax, which, under President Trump, was dropped to 21 percent from 35 percent. Biden has said he wants it hiked back to 28 percent. This could have a dramatic effect on the profitability of your investments as well as the health and competitiveness of our economy. However, I believe, this is not the biggest issue that could face the sensible investor.

What Happens to Your Retirement Accounts

Qualified retirement accounts, accounts that give you various tax breaks, have been used by millions of Americans and form the basis of much of their wealth. For instance, I have four retirement accounts and my wife has two. They now represent about sixty percent of our total wealth. They are a big reason why we are financially independent. Generally, they have been a big wealth creator for us and millions of others, both because of the tax breaks and because some of our employers provided us with generous matches. Remember, always take advantage of matches. All of these accounts have benefited since the crash of 2008 and the runup over the past four years has been considerable.

Until recently, Americans were allowed to put up to $6,500 a year in their IRAs ($7,000 if you are over age 50. The smart investor, unless he or she is convinced that premature death is near or is coming up on age 70, always puts in the maximum amount). But those numbers are likely going up as they do when there is inflation as there is almost every year. That's another reason why should always try to save a little more when you are trying to reach a goal.

There are also limits on how much one can put into his or her 401(k)-retirement plan at work. All those limits might be raised in a Biden administration or simply increase owing to cost-of-living adjustments. As inflation increases, limits are often raised.

When and if these savings, investment and business incentives take place—and I think it is likely that at least some of them will take place—wise investors should jump on them. In the era of Trump , he or she should remember these basic principles.

*Don't take the extra money and blow it on taking on more credit card debt: Get rid of this card debt forever.

*Take advantage of lower capital gains rates for as long as they last and when available and enjoy getting the most out of his or her gains, knowing he or she will keep more of them than before.

*Realize that lower taxes mean a greater opportunity to save and invest. Jump on them as you would a bargain in a discount store. Neither may not be there for long.

This could be the time when the intelligent investor takes giant steps toward financial independence.

But here is the dark side of these qualified retirement saving accounts. The government, barring some miracle, could be hard up for money in the near future. Some of our leaders have already indicated that they want to tax the "rich," but what does the latter mean?

Some of our pols have said would need "new revenues,"

new taxes, to follow their plans to remake the country. That means the government gets bigger and bigger as well as more centralized; that the federal government reduces the power of the 10th amendment to the U.S. Constitution, which reserves certain powers to the states. But where will they get the Biden administration get more money? They might seriously consider new taxes on these qualified retirement accounts.

By the way, in most cases, you are already paying taxes on these accounts when you start drawing them down. However, I fear that won't stop a ravenous government looking for more money. Indeed, we already pay taxes on these accounts when we start collecting at between ages 59.5 and about age 70. Right now, as I have advocated, you reduce taxation by taking minimum distributions.

Still, many of the tax reductions that have made these qualified retirement savings could come under attack as the Biden goes on a domestic spending spree. Watch for this development such as a new call to increase taxation on these trillions of dollars of accounts. Be sure to tell your legislators as well as organizations such as the AARP that you have already paid too much in taxes and not to touch these vital accounts. The latter, if sufficient, can help tens of millions of Americans live comfortably for the rest of their lives.

These accounts are critical to our lives. They are also essential to our nation's economy because they expand the savings pool, which lowers the interest rate. The latter means millions of people can finance a house, cars and new businesses because the price of money is low.

Your savings, retirement and otherwise, also help this country. They should be protected and expanded as much as possible for the nation's health, regardless of who is president. Indeed, I continue to slightly increase our retirement savings because I work part-time. And, since one of my retirement accounts is a Roth, I can put up to $7,000 of "earned" income in my account each year and I never have to touch it. I use other accounts to pay bill. The Roth keeps growing. It is a last line of our financial defense. This is one of the ways I believe that my wife and I will never run out of money.

In our last chapter, our last, we'll restate the central ideas in this book.

Financial Principles for the Rest of Your Life

In completing our plan for your financial health, let's review some of the most important ideas that we have discussed.

> *the smart investor understands the dangers of debt in an age of buy now, live big and forget about the future.*

Maybe this is the most important issue of all.

Why?

One must understand why it is very important not to be a revolver and always be a transactor. The former carries card balances from month to month, the latter pays off debts each month and avoids all credit card interest. If you don't understand and apply this lesson, you could wreck your life. You could spend years, maybe decades, trying to dig out from under debt. Let me cite an example.

A friend and I attended college at night in the 1970s. We both had full- time jobs in the day. I paid for college with cash. I stayed at home, worked during the day and went to college at night.

My friend fell for the university college loan pitch about the wonders of student loans. He took lots of them and also used credit cards to pay for college. By the way, here's one reason why people of my generation ended up with so much college debt. I remember at an orientation session in 1974 at my university, Fordham, which, by the way, is now a "woke" school. An official explained how easy it was to get student loans and how low the interest rate was. He practically begged us to take loans as though they were manna from heaven.

"But," a student asked, "suppose you don't need any student loans?"

The university official told the audience take them anyway and put the money in the bank, making money on "the differences in interest rates." However, my friend, and many of my other classmates took these loans as quickly and in as big amounts as they could. I didn't because I always thought something seemed fishy about these loans and because I thought I could just stay ahead of my college bills by working full-time during the day (An experience that, finally, taught me how hard my parents worked to support us in one of the most expensive cities in the world, especially when I realized how much in taxes was taken out each week).

My friend and I both began our post-college careers making small incomes, trying to establish ourselves in our respective professions. I had no debt. Therefore, I was able to begin saving small amounts even in my 20s when I was making very little. I saved and invested almost nothing, but luckily, I had neither credit card nor student loan debt. So I was able to pay for my used cars, purchased with cash. Later on, my wife and I, trying to get our first mortgage, were just able to get one even thought our total income was so-so. Why? We had no student loans and were paying off card debts almost every month.

An Almost Perpetual Debt

My friend, who earned somewhat more than me through most of his career, found it difficult to save. His loans ate up a large percentage of his salary. The problem was he was paying off cards and student loans for more than a quarter of a century!

Think of all the interest he was paying. Think of all the money he could have added to his savings and investments if he wasn't burdened by those debts for so long!

Whether it is student loans or credit card debt or car loans or even mortgage debt, remember: These debts represent future demands on your income and on your ability to save and invest. They are a mortgage on your current and future income. This debt, and other red ink, prevents you from getting ahead. Sure, if you get a high paying job someday, you can justify it.

However, often your income in your 20s is relatively modest because you are trying to take the first steps in a profession. Yes, you may need these student loans to obtain a college degree essential to obtaining many jobs, although many technical schools and community colleges can also provide training at much cheaper prices.

(An aside, my wife obtained a masters' degree in communications that she hardly used. But later in life, she went to a technical school to study airplane mechanics. I am proud to say that she earned two very important certificates, power plant and airframe. She then had a very successful and profitable career as a plane mechanic, one of the first women at Delta Airlines at JFK airport. The point is: Not everyone needs a four-year university degree. Indeed, given the outrageous costs of some universities, many young people shouldn't take student loans no matter how smooth talking is the university official. They should think carefully before they take on debt and think what their initial salaries will be once they obtain a degree).

If you must take a student loan, take as little as you need and not a cent more. Millions of young Americans, for example, start out their adult lives saddled with incredible amounts of college debts that they may never be able to pay.

Indeed, many major political candidates are promising that these loans will be forgiven. However, at any age but especially when you are young and aren't clear about how you will do in your profession, take on debt carefully. Don't let people like that repulsive Fordham University official soft soap you with the idea that "it's only student debt." Yes, the interest rates are relatively low, but they still expect you to pay it all back, despite President Biden's promises that student loan debt would be forgiven. And, by the way, student loan interest rates can go up.

Indeed, many financial professionals say that student loans should be taken in consideration with what a potential degree will earn a person over the course of a working life.

Use debt for the right reasons, such as building a business that you expect to sell someday for a big price. Have a plan to retire the debt quickly.

*Start Preparing for Financial Independence as Soon as You Can:

No matter how small it may seem at first, start saving and investing on a regular basis. The sooner you get into a regular habit, the more it becomes a part of your life. It will become something you can accept without even thinking about it. "Civilization advances by extending the number of important operations which we can perform without thinking about them," according to A.N. Whitehead as quoted in F.A Hayek's "The Constitution of Liberty."

An Automatic Pilot Taking You to Safe Harbor

Regular saving and investing means progress then happens every week or every pay check. As the years go by, you are getting closer and closer to your goal. The easiest way is to use the automatic, "I can't see it so I can't spend it" idea. Look at investing the same way you look at paying your bills each month. Have money taken out of your paycheck automatically and put it into your retirement accounts. That's the way many people pay their bills. Use the same technique for saving and investing.

Be sure the money gets to the investments; that it doesn't get waylaid by some impulse buying. Don't break into retirement accounts to pay for luxuries. Indeed, try to hold off using your retirement accounts as long as possible. Previously, I have detailed how breaking into retirement accounts is a disaster. It interrupts the compounding process.

Making contributions to retirement plans is doubly important if your employer will help; if he or she is providing you with a match or if the government is providing you with some sort of tax credit for retirement savings. Some people pass up these opportunities and almost always it is a huge mistake. They never contribute to company plans and never access the employer match. I've known people who never contributed to this kind of matching contribution retirement plan even though they had a very generous one at work. The most common excuse they told me was they "couldn't afford to do it."

That's almost always a big mistake. The truth is that they can't afford not to contribute if they ever expect to accrue enough money to become independent.

Why?

It will probably be their best, and possibly only, chance to build up a substantial nest egg.

Get all the employer matches and tax breaks you can and now. Keep getting them for as long as possible. Some day that employer won't be in your life so act today. The future is now.

It could be opportunity lost because many people work in companies that don't have generous saving and investing programs or in ones in which the retirement saving program is very little.

At the last full-time job I had, I was a reporter/editor with a small publishing firm for some 15 years. The employer, in my first ten years, offered a generous match on the 401(k) plan. Up to a six percent match. That meant every six percent you put up; it became twelve percent deposited in your account. Thank God I grabbed every cent.

After the crash of 2008, my employer was struggling to survive. The employer still offered a retirement plan but there was no longer an employer match. If you hadn't taken advantage of those matches in the previous 10 years, you couldn't go back and get them. They were gone, never to return. The weakened company was later sold. Thankfully, I was gone. I took my 401(k) money, which was close to a third of a million dollars, and put it into an IRA.

If you are at a company with a good match, take advantage of it now. You never know how long a generous program will last. These programs are usually based on the profitability of the company. If it suddenly runs into tough times, the company will reduce these programs.

This is also true with IRAs that provide tax breaks each year. The government, which goes deeper and deeper into the red each year, could very well reduce or even eliminate the deductibility of these savings programs.

Remember, while the IRA vehicle lasts, the amount you can contribute is often raised owing to inflation. Be sure to make the maximum contribution. And if you're putting money into an IRA, then put in the maximum amount and do it in January. Get the compounding process going for you as soon as possible.

Do it now. That's because you can't go back years later and recover these employer matches or tax breaks. They are there for you only today. They're gone tomorrow. Millions of Americans have literally passed up hundreds of billions, perhaps trillions, of dollars in matches and tax breaks over decades. What an incredible waste.

These people threw away money that could have helped them achieve financial independence, which can be a very important goal as you age. What does that mean?

Many Americans, with the higher taxes and other costs that are coming, just won't have enough dinero to walk away from unpleasant jobs or realize their freelance dreams in their 40s or 50s. Many will be stuck in jobs they hate. I don't want that to happen to any of my readers.

There's another reason why is it so important to accumulate a significant amount of savings and investment as soon as possible.

It's because, if you are a citizen of the United States or a Western European country, nations with a huge and growing welfare states, that it is likely taxes are already high. It is also likely that these taxes will go higher sometime in your lifetime. If you think I am exaggerating read the current Social Security Trustees report, which we have previously discussed. Bottom line: Cuts are coming for the program; either directly, benefit cuts, or indirectly through inflation.

Don't believe in pols, left or right, to take care of you. Take care of yourself. Believe in yourself, your religion, your family, friends, neighbors.

Higher taxes and a debased currency are as inevitable as corruption in big city political machines no matter who gets elected. This is true no matter which party is running things.

And part of these economic welfare state woes is due to a factor no pol can control: declining birth rates. That generates fewer taxpayers to pay for programs. That means a bigger tax bill for us. But the relentless overpromising of career pols of both parties, with a few exceptions, continues. It is the nature of career pols.

It's also because the United States, as well as almost every other advanced welfare state democracy, has huge unfunded entitlement obligations sometimes in the trillions of dollars at a time when fewer new workers are coming into the economy and old people are living longer and collecting for longer periods. It all adds up to a lot of red ink that we, the taxpayers, must pay.

For example, the United States' debt is already about some $36 trillion or so. (Emphasis on the word "about" in the last sentence. It seems to be going up every time Congress is in session. By the time you read this, it will probably a lot more as our pols continue their practice of buying votes in the runup to elections). However, I am skeptical about these self-assessed government numbers.

I'm not a conspiracy theory buff, but I don't believe the official government numbers. That's because the government is providing an unaudited number. It is, in effect, assessing and often gaming the system. Some independent authority should be adding up the numbers, not a government agency.

The debt, our debt, is a lot more than any official numbers and I see no reason why it won't go up a lot more in the future because very few career pols, of the left or the right, even think it is a problem or certainly not when they are running for office.

Neither governing party seems committed to anything but more spending no matter how self-destructive it is over the long term, even if it leads to long bout of inflation, an economic disease that can wreck millions of lives. Most our rulers both left and right are thinking about now and the next election cycle, not what is going to happen to your children and their children. Louis XV, the French king just before the French Revolution, knew that the country was heading toward financial disaster but he and his flunkies just kept on spending. Louis XV knew that problems were coming for France.

Indeed, the king was reputed to have said, as he and his minions were enjoying themselves as they overspent their citizens' hard-earned money, "Apres moi, le deluge." The deluge came. It was the French Revolution, which transformed the nation, and the world, in countless ways.

Le deluge possibly is coming soon for the advanced welfare state democracies unless dramatic changes come and happen soon. The Louis XV approach seems the usual way political parties win power in the advanced welfare democracy. They try to buy elections with promises, most of which are about as achievable as yours truly starting at second base for his beloved Bronx Bombers.

But more of the same will mean taxes, one way or another, will continue to rise. You'll need as much money as you can accumulate to pay for all this outrageous red ink that both left wing and right wing governments have accumulated over decades and will likely continue to do.

Prepare for the Worst

So you'll need lots of assets to retain a decent standard of living. Leave your retirement accounts alone unless it is an emergency. Let them compound as long as possible. Take advantage of them as long as possible, which means contribute to them as much as reasonably possible. This is very important.

At a retirement planning conference I attended about 20 years ago, a plan sponsor executive who helped employers set up private retirement plans made a plea: "Encourage and educate your employees to participate in these programs because, for many of them, it will be the only chance they have to amass significant assets."

Left unsaid: Please get your workers saving so they can avoid a very difficult retirement!

Don't stop with your retirement savings. Set up several different savings and investment techniques if you can. Remember you'll want some significant non-qualified assets to take advantage of retirement planning strategies we have previously outlined.

For example, have money taken out of your checking accounts and put into index funds. These are investments that can also compound over the long term and make a big difference in your life.

Remember not to rely on governments to take care of you. Take care of yourself. It can be done. It's not impossible even for middle-class people, who save a few hundred dollars a month and continue doing it over 20 or 30 years, to accumulate substantial amounts as we have shown in this book.

That's assuming your long-term rate of return is a modest eight or nine percent a year. Here are some smart money principles as we conclude our journey:

Small Is Much Better than None:

It is always better to light a candle than to curse the darkness. Sorry to repeat this phrase. However, I think there is endless wisdom in this simple idea. A beginning, no matter how small and seemingly insignificant, is a step in the right direction that can make a big difference over years. Later on, as you succeed in your profession and make more money, can increase your monthly saving rate.

But for now, get going. Take the first baby steps. Remember, just $100 a month into a fund that earns 12 percent a year will accumulate just under $1.2 million over 40 years. And $100 a month isn't beyond the reach of a lot of people. Indeed, I know people who spend $100 a month just on takeout coffee!

By the way, if you would rather curse the darkness for a few years before lighting a candle, consider this. If you waited for twenty years to start investing that $100 a month, that two-decade delay would make quite a difference. Putting $100 a month into an investment that earns 12 percent a year means you end up with about $100,000 over 20 years. That 20-year delay cost you $1.1 million! Just do now.

Take Care of Yourself Because You're Likely to Do the Best Job:

Yes, the government in most Western countries has some sort of pension/social security scheme aimed at helping you in old age. But remember: Most of these programs are not designed to be your primary source of income. They are intended to supplement private savings, which millions of Americans, young and old, lack. Besides, do you want to depend on a government-—any government left or right—to keep its promises and take care of you?

Governments have a tendency to "borrow" (sic) from these retirement funds. O.K. now I slipped into Orwellian Newspeak. Governments have a tendency to arrogate these funds. Our Social Security program is a lousy deal for most people and it could become even a worse one. I detailed the coming problems in a previous chapter.

Indeed, in the last presidential race a candidate actually said that Social Security payments may have to be "means tested." What would happen if that becomes a reality? Some people, who are believed to be well off, might someday not get any Social Security payments, or get less than promised, which will hurt their retirement plan assumptions. That's even though they had been forced to pay into the Social Security system for decades. Whether you are rich or poor, breaking promises is wrong.

Smart investors want to avoid this dependence on the promises of politicians, many of whom play games with the truth to get your vote, then contract amnesia after the election is over and they're ensconced in office.

Promises, Promises, Promises...

Here are just a few examples: In 1988, George H.W. Bush ran for office saying he would never raise taxes. He raised taxes. William Jefferson Clinton, four years after, ran for president saying he would enact a middle-class tax cut. It never happened. Bush's son, George W. Bush, ran in 2000 saying the United States should stop sending troops around the world and intervening in wars. He plunged the nation into a disastrous war in 2003. Barack Obama, in 2008, promised prosperity and to cut the deficit in half. Neither happened. I could go on and on with other ridiculous promises such as the Trump promises to end deficits, another laugh a minute at the expense of the already overburdened taxpayers. Biden always seems to be making incredible, impossible promises, in the true tradition of our political ruling class. Indeed, I just might go on and on about these lies in another book.

Inevitably, politicians, with their various schemes and their inability to admit that the surpluses were wrongly, and illegally, spent are talking about cutting back the program. Don't dismiss that last sentence. The original Social Security law of 1935 says Social Security benefits are not a contractual right. And the Nestor vs. Fleming U.S. Supreme Court decision of 1960 upheld that terrible principle. (It was decided on a 6-3 decision and some of the dissents in the court ruling are fascinating).

So, barring a miracle, this is inevitable: Those headed for retirement tomorrow and 20 years from now are likely to get much less than previous generations did from Social Security.

Some institutions studying Social Security rates of return are projecting that this generation, when it is ready to retire, will end up receiving a negative rate of return for its "contributions." Already, many of us are seeing that this program is gradually giving us less.

Personal aside: My wife, who wanted until age 70 to collect Social Security to get the higher payments, had modest incomes throughout her life. Now, through hard work and good investments, she and I have healthy assets. Through a good part of our lives we were part of the working poor, although it never bothered us. We just kept working.

However, now, unlike her grandmother, she will pay taxes on her Social Security payments. It is owing to how badly this system is run that she will now pay taxes on taxes. The same will soon happen to me. The same will happen to tens of millions of other Americans, who paid the payroll taxes for decades and now will pay more taxes.

Don't depend on this flawed Social Security program for a huge part of your retirement income. Try, as much as you can, to depend on yourself. So be sure you have private savings and investments. The latter have a quality that is important at any age. You, not some government administrator, control them and how they will be spent.

Why the Wise Investor Saves and Invests:

What is the point of following rational spending and investing policies; of being the Tacano in your family?

It is, in a phrase, financial independence. The guiding philosophy is: The best thing that money can provide isn't necessarily a possession—such as a big house, car or great vacations or a showy display of high living. Those are all nice things for some. If they are important to you, you should try to achieve them, again with the provision that you can pay for them.

But there's something much better than any one possession can provide: It is the peace of mind that comes from knowing that you have enough so you don't have to depend on Social Security or any government program or any employer for a substantial part of your income as unfortunately millions of Americans do.

It comes from feeling good about not having to take a wretched, but possibly high-paying, job that will make you, and probably your family as well, miserable. You don't need that job. You have significant savings and investments that were accumulated over decades of commonsense spending, saving and investing practices that you put on automatic pilot early in your life.

It comes from turning your back on a job at a company that is running down—turning your back on the job because you know you don't need it anymore. How does one achieve that freedom?

It comes from arriving at a state that the novelist Dostoevsky called "coined freedom."

My wife and I achieved that. It took a few years, but I can tell you it is a great feeling; a kind of liberation knowing you don't have to squeeze on to that wretched crowded E-train or drive carefully on that jammed highway to get to work. Peace of mind, not possessions per se, is the best thing to keep your blood pressure in an acceptable range and make these the best years of your life.

Dear Readers, I wish you all the best.

Appendix: A Chapter on Economic History

Prepare for Big Spending Money Mischief; the Inevitability of Tax Increases.

The Right Way to Get Out of a Depression or Recession

Throughout this book I have emphasized the need for extensive preparation in achieving financial independence. In part it is because people are living longer, and that means they'll need a lot more money than previous generations.

Most people understand that. However, what I think many people don't comprehend is that their government, which is a growing welfare/warfare state, is running up incredible debts and has been doing so for decades regardless of which party was in power. So, citizens will ultimately pay for this in various painful ways, including economic woes such as more recessions and more depressions. Unfortunately, most of our political leaders seem to think that—whether dealing with health or economic problems or turning around the business cycle—the way out of every problem is spending more and more. They're setting a bad example for Americans.

Individuals can't spend their way out of money problems by taking on more debt to escape debt is a central theme of this book. But neither can governments, even though they have printing presses and can require people to use their devalued money. Our federal government's long-term reckless spending and taxing policies—implicitly or explicitly backed by most members of Congress—impoverish Americans. They also psychologically cripple many Americans as more and more Americans think only the government can save them.

Spending Big and Handing You the Bills

Congressional leaders, many of whom have already passed several stimulus packages, debate more of the same as a way of pulling the nation out of impending economic problems. Typical of this thinking U.S. House of Representatives Democrats offered another stimulus measure during the height of the Covid crisis.

"We must think big for the people now," said House of Representatives Speaker Nancy Pelosi a few years ago. "Not acting is the most expensive course," speaking of her $3 trillion dollar legislation.

The package was contained in an 1,815-page document submitted to Congress. It included more spending on almost everything. It was approved by the House with little review in three days. Later another spending package was offered of almost 6,000 pages and lawmakers had to vote on it in about ninety minutes.

GOP no Better than the Dems

The leaders of the Republican Senate have said some of these packages were "dead on arrival." However, the Republican opposition is not philosophical; it is political.

The GOP, which already helped pass several stimulus bills, was recently working on its own new package. They basically have the same idea: Only more government spending solves the economic problem and forget about the dangers of long-term debt. That's even though previous flawed government policies caused the problem, hurting countless many small businesses. And remember more debt inevitably mean more taxes and more government controls.

Still, most members of Congress argue that they deserve more "emergency" powers and should be able to spend much more. These kinds of policies have been explained in the book "Crisis and Leviathan; Critical Episodes in the Growth of American Government" by Robert Higgs.

It documents how emergencies, or quasi emergencies, result in more government powers. "Once constitutional barriers have been lowered during a crisis," he writes, "a legal precedent has been established giving government greater potential for expansion in subsequent non-crisis periods, particularly those that can be plausibly described as crises."

These policies lead to many questions but perhaps the most relevant is: Who will pay for this?

These spending bills add enormous costs to an already bulging debt. But pump priming is exactly what was advocated by the most influential and destructive economist of the 20th century, John Maynard Keynes. He claimed to be an opponent of socialism but argued for "the socialism of investment." Governments, he wrote, should spend to keep the economy booming. This ignores the dangers of overspending: Bubbles, resulting crashes, and the seemingly constant justification of more government spending.

How Much More Debt? Who Knows?

Today that means that the already red ink plagued America continues and expands deficit spending and debts. Before this crisis started, America's debt was "officially" $24 trillion" and it has obviously gone up. Even the recent $24 trillion figure was a dubious number since the government doesn't impose the standards of the GAAP (The Generally Accepted

Accounting Standards) that it requires of private firms. Today it's obviously a lot more but how much more?

So what is the true amount of debt?

"That is a good question," says Garrett Watson, a senior analyst, with the Mercatus Center at George Mason University. He says the debatable issue is whether to count all the future promises governments have made over decades for programs such as Social Security and Medicare.

The debt of the United States recently topped $26 trillion for the first time, according to a June 2020 report of the United States Treasury Department, but it has gone up much more since then. The report also said the debt had topped $24 trillion only two months before. It's gone up a lot since then and will probably do some more since there are few lawmakers---Republican or Democrat—who seem to worry about overspending on the debasement of the currency. As I write this, late in 2024, the "official" debt is some $36 trillion, which again I think is a fraudulent number.

Fudging the Numbers

But there are many who question these official numbers and say they are much worse. People debate how deep the debt is. Some are skeptical observers, such as economist Laurence Kotlikoff. He contends that the government numbers are fraudulent. He says the government is a "functional bankrupt." He says that it couldn't pay off if most, or even a significant number of, creditors all demanded payment. That has happened to some banks that failed

Kotlikoff's views government debt as similar to the way fractional reserve banking works. In the latter, if a large number of depositors all want their money at the same time, the banking system collapses. And, as the debt obligations of the U.S. government continue to rise, if a large number of creditors all cash in their treasuries at the same time, or if many investors stop buying treasuries, then the government would default, Kotlikoff says.

The founders of the United States understood the problem because they lived through it. That's because many of them had made the mistake of overissuing currency to try to pay for the Revolutionary War. Later, in the writing of the Constitution, James Madison wrote of the "pestilent effects of paper money." Madison and others who wrote the constitution hoped that their insistence on hard money, which is specie or gold and silver, would avoid another outbreak of what was often the result of paper money: devaluation and robbery.

But this money devaluation and robbery has already happened in our lifetimes. Today's expanding debts and currency overissue could give us a rehash of the 1970s. Then the value of dollars drastically declined because of deficits and the over creation of dollars. Cheap money also was part of the 2008 crash.

Today we see similar conditions. The government is spending trillions more that it doesn't have. Congress and the president pressure the central bank to keep interest rates at historically low levels. The Federal Reserve Bank is creating many new, devalued, dollars. It is spending the nation into a potential disaster. It is one in which tomorrow's taxpayers will be put in a terrible situation.

Getting Worse Over Decades

This is a problem that has been hanging over Americans for decades. For instance, ten years ago the official debt number was $13.4 trillion, according to the Congressional Budget Office (CBO). Back then many were speculating that the actual figure was much, much higher. Like a shopaholic who hides his or her credit card bills, the government pretends certain obligations and expenditures don't exist. Uncle Sam really owes closer to $60 trillion, or more, and the country is close to bankruptcy, several economists told me then in a story I did a decade ago.

"The government is lying about the amount of debt," Kotlikoff says. He is an economist at Boston University and co-author of "The Coming Generational Storm: What You Need to Know about America's Economic Future." He charged that the government "is engaging in Enron accounting."

The problem is simple: The government, at the urging of career politicians seeking to win elections and oblivious to the long-term effects of their spending policies, seeks to buy votes through impossible election promises. They spend too much but most of them—the career pols, most of whom have never worked in the private sector—win their elections.

A History of Reckless Government

Why does this reckless approach to the nation's economic health go on and on, despite occasional calls from those out of power to end it?

Politics.

It is the desire of career politicians, of both parties, to get elected and re-elected. More spending is often viewed as the elixir that will win elections.

It is a case of the short term versus the long term. The spending recklessness is because the vast majority of elected officials, both left and right, see relentless spending as politically advantageous. That's even though it is a destructive long-term practice. The basic problem of politics is the short term—the next election—versus the long term, a sensible economic policy whose benefits require discipline and aren't apparent for many years. That is very similar to the strategies that we have outlined in these pages for how an average person can become financially independent. He or she ensures one always keeps spending under control. He or she takes the long view and reaches financial independence over the long term.

But the spend without any limits government policy appeals to politicians of all stripes. It also appeals to credulous voters. Many continue to believe, despite evidence to the contrary, that the government will give them valuable services for nothing or very little. (Think of the condition of the roads, of public enterprises such as subways, Amtrak, public schools etc. Are the taxpayers and citizens getting value for their money? That's a rhetorical question). But now these big spending policies are going beyond bad economics. Today, the big spending ways of our politicians are, once again, endangering the economy.

A recent Government Accountability Office (GAO) report, in effect, blames both parties. It notes debt has gone from some $5 trillion to $24 trillion over 25 years. This was a time of both Republican and Democratic presidents and Republican and Democratic Congresses.

How Long Will It Continue?

But the always spend more idea, whether under presidents Obama or Trump or Biden, is starting to have a long-term destructive effect as the GAO and other government reports document. These big spending levels can't continue, according to a government spending watchdog.

These debts and deficits are "unsustainable," a report says.

That is the assessment of "The Nation's Fiscal Health," a GAO report. It was prepared just before trillions of dollars in new stimulus money were authorized by almost all Republicans and Democratic lawmakers in Congress as well as President Trump. The report warns these spending levels can't continue because of entitlement spending promises.

"While spending on Social Security already exceeds $1 trillion per year, health care and net interest are expected to grow faster than GDP and be key drivers of federal spending in the future. Medicare spending is projected to reach $1 trillion per year by 2026, and net interest is projected to hit this milestone by 2032," according to the GAO.

You Pay. We Give You Nada

Today, we not only have unprecedented levels of red ink, but there is a greater danger: A huge part of it will end up paying for nothing. It will leave the nation with a perpetual debt that compounds forever.

"Over the past 50 years, net interest costs have averaged 2 percent of GDP but these costs are projected to increase to 7.2 percent by 2049, when they become the largest category of spending," according to the GAO.

There is no doubt that the United States is headed for some hard times over the next decade or so unless someone—one or both of the major political parties or a backlash from tens of millions of American taxpayers—changes the reckless spending of our government. Already, over the last few years, we have seen a preview of the future as the government, several times under presidents of both parties, has had to raise the debt level. It is as if you have reached the limits of our credit cards, but Visa and MasterCard keep sending you letters telling you that you are a wonderful customer so they have extended your spending limits. You never stop to consider the consequences of your actions----the 20 percent or more you pay in interest or card. A friend just signed up for a new credit card with all sorts of rewards, except for one thing the card company didn't emphasize. If you were a revolver, you paid 30 percent interest---you just keep spending more.

As this book was being written, the nation, once again, is in the middle of still another economic crisis. This kind of crisis will continue for many years in part because the government has taken a bigger role in trying to cure the problem. This is ironic since many of the problems were created owing to bad government policies, including more and more spending, which is usually politically motivated.

These crises are why the smart investor constantly needs to overprepare for achieving financial independence. If you think you need a million to achieve it, go for one and half million. If you need two million dollars, try for three. Remember the Eisenhower rule we discussed earlier. In war or in retirement, always have more, much more, than you think you need.

Why over prepare?

The problem is that the government, whether right or left, continues to make the same mistakes that many overspending Americans are making.

GOP Is Generally no Better than the Dems

These spending today and forget about tomorrow policies lead to many questions but perhaps the most relevant is: Who will pay for all this?

But this money devaluation and robbery has already happened in our lifetimes. Today's debts and currency overissue could give us a rehash of the 1970s. Then the value of dollars drastically declined because of deficits and the over creation of dollars. Cheap money also was part of the 2008 crash.

Today we see similar conditions. The government is spending trillions more dollars that it doesn't have. Congress and the president pressure the central bank to keep interest rates at historically low levels. The Federal Reserve Bank is creating many new, devalued, dollars. It is spending the nation into a potential disaster. It is one in which tomorrow's taxpayers will be put in a terrible situation. The Fed, at some point, will have to drastically raise interest rates to break the back of inflation. In the process, the Fed of today, the same as the Fed of the late 1970s and early 1980s, will impose a painful recession on the nation.

A History of Reckless Government

Why does this reckless approach to the nation's economic health go on and on, despite occasional calls from those out of power to end it?

Politics. It is the desire of career politicians, of both parties, to get elected and re-elected. Spending is often viewed as the elixir that will win elections. But the voters must take some blame too. They're like junkies in the novel "Brave New World" who will do anything just as long as you give them more and more devalued dollars. In "Brave New World," the government keeps the citizens docile by providing them with more and more soma, a drug that keeps them in line. Today some governments see the virtues of pot: It believes it will put more money in their pockets.

It is a case of the short term versus the long term. The spending recklessness is because the majority of elected officials, both left and right, see relentless spending as politically advantageous. That's even though it is a destructive long-term practice.

The spend without any limits policy appeals to politicians of all stripes. But now it is going beyond bad economics. Some see it as a way to central planning.

Some, such as now former New York Governor Cuomo and now lame duck President Biden, talk about this crisis as a way to "restructure" American society. (And ensure their party holds on to power? This is a familiar strategy. President Trump was spending tons of money when he was running for re-election in 2020. It seems to be a given for every public official who wants to hang on to power or gain power by promising everything to everyone no matter how dishonest many of these promises are).

However, more commonly, overspending has been part of politics as usual in good times and bad. Spend lots of money and keep doing it, especially around election time. Forget any long-term effects. This is a strategy that has been tried before. It seems to succeed in the short term. But it creates a Potemkin Village effect. It looks good for a while until market players spot what has happened.

"I Did It...No, I Did It"

More spending is also often a political winner with people with short memories; people who spurn history and forget the long-term economic results of the big government. It is tantamount to using drugs. Initially, it feels great. But you have to keep taking drugs to ensure the high continues. To keep getting high, you have to take more and more drugs. Later you're hung over. And possibly you did major long-term damage to your body.

The United States Government Could Become a Giant Revolver

The United States, on the present course, could become another Weimar Republic or possibly just have another painful deep recession as it did in 2008. If it continues on its present Keynesian course, the nation will have the same problem as millions who mismanage credit cards. They face a perpetual debt. They can only pay interest on cards monthly. They can never get at the principal. They face debts that could ruin them.

The credit card industry has a term for these beloved customers. It is "revolvers." As we discussed previously, they are those cardholders who have revolving credit lines. They pay interest each month to the delighted card companies.

The United States, due to its huge welfare/warfare state philosophy, is a nation whose government is a giant revolver. It can never even reduce or retire its debt or even have a year in which it doesn't add to it since it always has deficits. This collective red ink—the deficit of each year added to the permanent debt—is destroying the nation, according to the GAO.

However, the danger is deeper, more dangerous, than economic. It is philosophic. Many are unconsciously using the big spending philosophy to move the nation to socialism. They believe that the "benefits" of government spending, of government taking more and more of our assets as well as those of future generations, will restore prosperity.

The policy may seem harmless. Some even say it is beneficial. But it is destroying liberty and long-term prosperity. But in the short term the policy often seems wonderful and pols often take bows for policies that are actually horrendous.

The Roots of an American Socialism

Over close to a century each generation has been depending on the government more and more and on themselves less and less. At the same time, they have seen major political parties gradually move more and more to socialism, ideas that would have stunned predecessors. That's because they now agree with former U.S. House of Representatives Speaker Nancy Pelosi: Only the government, not individuals, can turn things around.

Yet once the standard government policy for reversing bad economic times was the opposite: The government facing a depression would let economies naturally recover without stimulus packages and other government interventions. Administrations as varied and distant as Martin Van Buren in 1837, Grover Cleveland in 1892 and Warren Harding in the early 1920s held to these principles. Some Democratic presidents, including the Kennedy and Truman administrations, also didn't use budget-busting stimulus packages but cut taxes as a way of helping the economy recover. In the case of Truman, the tax cut was passed over his veto by a Republican Congress. In the case of Kennedy, he changed his thinking and embraced tax cuts. That Kennedy volte-face is something that many Democrats today don't want to acknowledge.

However. the standard policy of letting economies naturally recover from depression, of cutting taxes, was reversed in the administration of President Herbert Hoover—accurately called by one historian, Joan Hoff Wilson, as a "Forgotten Progressive"—and also by the succeeding administrations of President Franklin Roosevelt and others. FDR took the Hoover approach of the government pumping up the economy and expanded it. That's even though FDR's supporters and most mainstream historians have wrongly branded Hoover a laissez-faire president. So for many years the lesson of letting market forces cure depression has been forgotten or condemned as a return to the policies of Herbert Hoover.

The government now seems forever committed to promoting booms. Leon Levy, a founding chairman of Oppenheimer & Co., called Keynes "the most influential economist of the 20th century." He was right. Levy, by the way, agreed with Keynes that high savings rates were bad for the economy. Writing in 2002, in his book "The Mind of Wall Street," he warned that, if the nation's savings rate rose above the six percent to ten percent range, "the country will be in deep trouble." But I'm sure Levy, an influential Wall Street player, had a personal savings rate of lot more than six to ten percent of his personal income.

This anti-saving prejudice is wrong. Indeed, it was. John Templeton invested heavily in Asian economies in the late part of last century. He believed their strong savings rates were in part why these countries achieved strong growth rates. But that view contrasted with the most influential economist of our time.

The Economist of Economists

John Maynard Keynes wrote that governments should create and then permanently sustain booms by its spending and monetary policies.

"The right remedy for the trade cycle is not to be found in abolishing booms and thus keeping us permanently in a semi-slump; but in abolishing slumps and thus keeping us in a quasi-boom," according to Keynes' most influential work, "The General Theory."

That was written in the midst of the Great Depression of the 1930s. Many of its ideas were more extensively applied in the administrations of President Franklin Delano Roosevelt, although key FDR advisers such as Marriner Eccles were convinced of this course even before they read Keynes and before they put FDR's New Deal policies into effect.

The result was FDR and his advisors, despite inflationary Keynesian policies and historical myths today, never restored prosperity. But most people didn't understand this because the nation was plunged into war toward the end of FDR presidencies, presidencies that are revered by many. President Biden was in the process of using those same FDR policies recently , but on a far bigger scale. He even likes to compare himself to FDR. But like FDR, it is simply a fact that, despite his considerable spending, FDR never restored the prosperity of the 1920s.

"Whatever it (the New Deal) was, it was not a recovery program, or, at any rate, not an effective one." writes David M. Kennedy in his book "Freedom from Fear," a history of the Great Depression. But hagiographic FDR biographers like Conrad Black ignore the economic evidence of failure and instead focus on FDR the successful politician. (He was. He was elected four times, even though those close to him knew he would never survive a fourth term. But like today's career pols, FDR was a flawed economic thinker.

Indeed, FDR, an incredibly popular president and superb politician elected four times, was unfortunately not a profound economic thinker (FDR once had meeting with Keynes and came away confused, thinking Keynes was a mathematician). Nevertheless, FDR used Keynesian policies adopted for the United States, but they failed.

By the late 1930s, James Farley, a key FDR advisor and postmaster general, was warning that things were even worse than under Hoover. That was one of the reasons why Farley, once one of the president's close political advisors, parted with the president when he ran for a third term in 1940. FDR had been guided by the ideas of Keynes even if he didn't quite understand them.

"Keynes," wrote the economist Benjamin Anderson, "was a dangerously unsound thinker. He believed that purchasing power or consumption---not production or saving---was the key to a strong economy." One often hears echoes of Keynes today when mainstream media often say that the consumer is 60 percent or 70 percent of the economy, ignoring the importance of production (saving and investment. Without that, there would be a lot fewer consumers. To me, saving is delayed consumption, which is why saving, pace Keynes, is good).

Keynes was dangerous because his theories, whether understood or not by most lawmakers, gave them intellectual license to spend and tax without limits; to ignore the classical liberal ideas of limited government. Hundreds of our leaders loved these statist ideas.

Keynes argued that supply doesn't create demand so the government, through spending, must prop up or create demand. Keynes didn't believe that a recovery through the natural reduction of prices and the increase in productivity was the right course. That's even through that formula worked just a decade or so before as we will later see.

Keynes and His Slaves

Keynes' influence in the Roosevelt administration "was very great," Anderson writes in "Economics and the Public Welfare." Most of FDR's political allies endorsed Keynes without reading his books.

We must create a boom by spending trillions of dollars is the Pelosi/Keynes philosophy.

Today the vast majority of our leaders are following this same quasi-socialist, spend the country back to prosperity, road even though few of them have ever read Keynes. Most Republicans and Democrats, share a tacit bi-partisan prejudice in favor of bigger government. They believe fiscal and monetary policies can artificially create "quasi booms," the language of Keynes.

The economist's dense writings are rarely read by our rulers. Yet his influence is felt more than 75 years after his death. This is ironic. Keynes famously wrote, "Practical men, who believe themselves to be quite exempt from any intellectual influences, are usually the slaves of some defunct economist." Keynes has been dead for over three quarters of a century, yet his theories still rule over many leaders, whether they know so or it.

Many of our career politicians, few of whom have ever studied Keynes, insist the way out of this economic disaster is more of the same.

More than Economics

FDR's questionable big spending policies, which are very similar to the stimulus policies advocated today by many Democrats and Republicans, never cured the Great Depression.

Some of Keynes supporters now concede that these policies have previously failed but they argue that not enough spending was employed. With more spending, they argue, they will succeed. And some of them now advocate these big spending policies as a "way to re-structure" our nation. Left unsaid by many of our popular politicians: This is another way of quietly giving Americans a "socialism without doctrines."

These self-destructive policies also ignore history.

They advocate dysfunctional economic policies that will fall upon you and your children. These policies don't create prosperity, yet they are often politically popular when pushed by some politicians. This explains why FDR, despite flawed economic policies that never pulled America out of a depression and restored the strong economy of most of the 1920s, was re-elected three times and is revered by millions of Americans as the man who supposedly saved America.

Yet the Bidden/FDR policies cripple Americans They will hurt our country even more tomorrow because they ignore basic economic principles. The more money government takes out of peoples' pockets, the more money that is taking out of production—savings and investment—the more difficult it is for the economy to grow. It is more than economics. It is philosophy. But it is an economics and philosophy that many Americans have forgotten or never heard.

Economics and History 101

When the government spends more, it takes away more of our economic liberty. It creates long term misery.

When it spends less, a lot less, it engages in a kind of Gladstonian thrift. Then we not only have more liberty and keep more of our hard-earned dollars, we prosper.

This seems like a ridiculously simple idea. Yet it is the opposite of a once bi-partisan economic policy that over generations was the standard for escaping economic woes. Today's Keynesianism—and Keynes was contemptuous of Gladstonian thrift and middle-class values just as today's collectivists often demean middle class values—ignores or denigrates the Anglo-American classical liberal traditions.

W.E. Gladstone, a British 19th century prime minister and before that a great Chancellor of the Exchequer, argued state spending and various government schemes would not save the citizen. He once aimed to abolish the income tax because he was suspicious of the power of governments to pry into people's lives.

"Of one thing I am, and am always been convinced—it is not by the State that man can be regenerated and the terrible woes of this darkened world effectually dealt with," said Gladstone, a very religious man who often attended several sermons on Sunday and was a close friend of the great Catholic historian of freedom Lord Acton. (Acton is a favorite of mine. That's because, as he grew older, he never became conservative. He became more radical for liberty).

Gladstone, much to his credit, quit his last ministry in 1894 because he opposed "constructionism" (socialism), big increases in military spending and was frustrated that parliament would not grant home rule to Ireland, which later rebelled in the middle of the First World War. It is in Ireland that Gladstone wanted to help remedy the injustices of centuries of English rule.

Gladstone also thought overspending was ill-moral. "The Peoples' William" would go around 10 Downing Street putting out unneeded candles and fireplaces. He thought that all wasteful government spending was wrong. He believed government surpluses should be returned to taxpayers, and that taxes should be as low possible. This was a Jeffersonian idea.

In his first administration in 1801, President Jefferson, rejecting the taxes of the previous Federalist administration, warned that "a wise and frugal government" should leave citizens "free to regulate their own pursuits on industry and improvement, and shall now take from the mouth of labor the bread it has earned. This is the sum of good government."

These were principles many of our own lawmakers once followed because most Americans believed them. But the idea of letting people keep the fruits of their labors, of the government not interfering with the natural recovery of economies through market forces, isn't so distant.

Indeed, just over a century ago that economics of liberty not only allowed an economy to recover but to prosper. And it happened about a century ago.

Harding, Silent Cal, Mellon and the Unknown Depression

A year or so after the conclusion of World War I, U.S. officials found themselves in a bleak position. The federal debt had exploded because of wartime expenditures. Annual consumer price inflation rates had increased more than 20 percent by the end of the war. The unemployment rate peaked at

11.7 percent in 1921.The same year, the new president, Warren Harding, promised to restore the traditional laissez-faire philosophy

How had America arrived at the depression of 1920? Today's leaders might consider these words.

"Business was depressed. For months following the Armistice we had persisted in a course of much extravagance and reckless buying. Wages had been paid out that had not been earned. The whole country, from the national government down had been living on borrowed money," wrote Calvin Coolidge, Harding's taciturn vice president, in his autobiography. Coolidge credits a regime of spending reductions and tax cuts for turning the economy around.

The depression of 1920-21 is a little known one yet it would be the last one in which primarily laissez-faire methods would be used to reverse it. The economy was allowed to naturally recover. Most people have never heard of it. That's because it was a depression that was short; about 18 months. It was one in which market forces generally operated and one in which they led to a strong recovery.

The Cycles of History

Just about a century ago America's economic situation was grim. In 1920, unemployment had jumped from 4 percent to nearly 12 percent, GNP declined 17 percent and American along with the rest of the West, was just getting over the Spanish Flu, which had killed millions. Secretary of Commerce Herbert Hoover—falsely characterized as a supporter of laissez-faire economics—urged President Harding to consider an array of government interventions to turn the economy around that Nancy Pelosi probably would have endorsed.

Hoover was ignored. Harding didn't go along with him.

The Cure for Unemployment

Warren Harding, whose administration later was caught up in the Teapot Dome scandal, laid out a series of laissez faire principles at the outset of his administration that worked.

"We will attempt intelligent and courageous deflation, and strike at government borrowing which enlarges the evil, and we will attack high cost of government with every energy and facility which attend Republican capacity. We promise that relief which will attend the halting of waste and extravagance, and the renewal of the practice of public economy, not alone because it will relieve tax burdens but because it will be an example to stimulate thrift and economy in private life," Harding said in a 1920 speech. It was very unlike the policies of most of his successors who faced similar economic woes.

Harding called "for denial and sacrifice, if need be, for a nationwide drive against extravagance and luxury, to a recommittal to simplicity of living, to that prudent and normal plan of life which is the health of the republic. There hasn't been a recovery from the waste and abnormalities of war since the story of mankind was first written." He also warned that "needless spending and heedless extravagance have marked every decay in the history of nations."

Harding's words should be considered in the light of warnings from today's Congressional watchdogs that, if current spending patterns continue, interest on the debt will someday soon become the biggest item in the budget. That would have repulsed Harding and Coolidge, whose approach was very different from today's big spending policies of most Democrats and Republicans in Congress and presidents who have forgotten the recovery efforts of a Kennedy or a Reagan.

No Government Big Spending

In 1921, there was no massive stimulus spending and the inflationary ideas of a Keynes, although there was an attempt to do so by Hoover. Malinvestments were liquidated as the government didn't rush in to rescue failing politically connected business.

This is a key element in any strong recovery as detailed by economist Joseph Schumpeter in the book "Business Cycles." He argued that, in a depression and a recovery, malinvestments must be allowed to liquidate. The economy, he argued, must be cleansed if a strong recovery is to happen. If you interrupt the cleansing process, Schumpeter argued, you stop the recovery. The depression continues as it did under both Hoover and FDR. Neither restored a strong economy unless you count war, and its horrors it brings even to the "winning" side, as an effective strategy for a healthy economy.

Cut Everything

So, instead of "fiscal stimulus," Harding strongly cut government spending between 1921 and 1922. The rest of Harding's approach was largely laissez-faire. Tax rates were slashed for all income groups. The national debt was reduced by one-third. More importantly, markets were allowed to operate. Wages and price drops took effect as the market corrected itself.

Austrian economist Murray Rothbard, in "America's Great Depression," says the Harding government did tinker with the economy through monetary policy; the easing of interest rates. However, Rothbard also noted that wage rates were "permitted to fall, and government expenditure and taxes were reduced." Rothbard says this was "our last natural recovery to full employment."

"The old-fashioned" approach prevailed in the recovery from the depression. "Government, the older view which had been the standard many times before, should keep taxation and spending low and reduce the public debt. Unemployment dropped to 6.7 percent by 1922, and was down to 2.4 percent by 1923.

"In 1920-21," economist Benjamin Anderson writes in "Economics and the Public Welfare," "we took our losses, we readjusted our financial structure, we endured our depression, and in August 1921 we started up again. By the spring of 1923 we had reached new highs in industrial production and we had labor shortages."

"The Best Treasury Secretary Since Alexander Hamilton"

President Harding was aided by a Treasury Secretary who followed the old-fashioned policies, Andrew Mellon. His book, "Taxation: The Peoples Business," is a treasury of commonsense and limited government. He contended government should be run on business principles. This is a fascinating exposition of Mellon's low taxation ideas.

Mellon warned high taxes not only hurt the rich, but the poor as well because taxes embedded in items drive up the cost of living for everyone. Indeed, I see the same happening today when I go shopping. And high tax rates tend to produce higher prices for the everyday items that most people buy. High tax rates, he added, are counterproductive for the government. That's because, Mellon wrote, higher rates often generate less, not more, tax revenue.

Federal taxation, he argued, "should be the least burden to the people" and "yielding the most revenue to the government." The way to do the latter was through low taxes. For instance, he contended that high capital gains taxes, estate and gift taxes ultimately hurt the government. In the long run, they produce lower revenues.

Mellon also warned that regressive taxes inevitably led citizens into tax shelters, which was not good for the economy or the government's efforts to raise money. He disliked municipal bonds. Most people bought them because tax rates were too high, he said. So they were looking for tax relief, but they were not putting money into productive businesses that would help the economy grow, according to Mellon.

Mellon: Get Rid of War Taxes

Everyone, most especially average people without any investments and those who wanted the government to receive as big revenues as possible, was better off with low taxation, Mellon contended.

Reviewing the high tax rates of World War I, including the surtaxes aimed at great wealth, Mellon wrote that "Experience has shown that the present high rates of surtax are bringing in each year progressively less revenue to the government." But he noted the secondary effects of these taxes were hurting more than the rich.

"High taxation, even if levied upon an economic basis, affects the prosperity of the country, because in its ultimate analysis the burden of all taxes rests only in part upon the individual or the property taxed. It is largely borne by the ultimate consumer. High taxation means a high price level and high cost of living." Mellon brilliantly concludes that a reduction in taxes helps everyone.

After his initial work in 1921-22, Mellon also followed with more tax cuts throughout the rest of the decade. This sparked a boom that carried into the next administration. The prosperity resulted in members of Congress calling Mellon "the best Treasury Secretary since Alexander Hamilton."

Mellon's tax cuts policies were also used by the post-World War II Federal Republic of Germany's Finance Minister, Ludwig Erhard. His low tax policies after World War II led to "the German economic miracle." About a decade after the creation of the German Federal Republic, Germany's living standards had surpassed social democratic Britain.

Indeed, by the mid-1970s, a British prime minister, comparing the post-World War II growth rates of the two countries, concluded, "We just think we won World War II." The post-World War II Labour government had enacted skimpy tax cuts, fearful some people would get rich while the jovial Erhard slashed taxes deeply in the German Federal Republic. He didn't fear people getting the rich. They point of good fiscal and monetary policy is for as many people as possible to have better lives, which is the point of this book.

Harding also called for people to adopt thrift. Meanwhile, Hoover, with his calls for big government spending as part of a counter cyclical approach to recovery, made little headway in the Harding administration. In the succeeding presidency, President Calvin Coolidge virtually held Hoover in contempt. He privately complained that every piece of advice that he had received from him had been wrong. By contrast, Coolidge praised the Mellon policies that had reversed the depression of 1920-1921.

"Within a year the country had adopted that course, which has brought an era of great plenty," Coolidge wrote.

Hoover and Harding

However, the boom times of the 1920 came to a crashing end when the Mellon philosophy was ended and Hoover became president in 1929. Hoover's embrace of disastrous high tariff policies combined with terrible central bank decisions suddenly condemned the nation to continued depression. Interestingly, we face both possibilities today. Now that Hoover was president, he finally adopted the stimulus, anti-depression policies that had been dismissed by the Harding administration 1921-1922. Hoover sacked Mellon, also raised taxes and tried to bail out several failing companies, not allowing the malinvestments to die. These policies are similar to those being used today by both our major political parties to avoid depression. Sometimes they are used even when times are good; in order to "keep the boom going," which is a quote from Keynes.

Later, when Hoover was president, he would be the first president to ignore laissez faire policies and apply government stimulus in a depression. In his memoirs, he bragged about it.

"No government in Washington has hitherto considered that it held so broad a leadership in such times," Hoover wrote in his memoirs. Indeed, he claimed that, "for the first time in the history of depression, dividends, profits and the cost of living have been reduced before wages have suffered." True, but the country continued in depression in the Hoover and the FDR years.

Hoover was ignoring something that many of today's leaders also do: High wages aren't any good when you're out of work.

Hoover, Rothbard writes, should be "considered the founder of the New Deal in America." He also disdained Mellon's advice and eventually exiled him to England as ambassador. What did Mellon advocate when the U.S. went into another depression, a depression that would last much longer than 1920-21 and one incorrectly blamed on laissez-faire policies?

Mellon's Exile and Prosecution

Mellon argued for letting malinvestments liquidate and for tax cuts. In other words, repeat what had been done in 1920-1921. His advice was ignored. Hoover actually raised taxes in the middle of a depression as would the succeeding president, Franklin Delano Roosevelt. These were incredibly unsuccessful policies and I fear that President Biden, for political reasons and owing to an ignorance of economic history, may follow them.

The government, Mellon believed, should not rescue badly run firms. But the Reconstruction Finance Corp. (RFC), set up by Hoover, was a government corporation designed to save struggling businesses. So, the government propping up the economy idea wasn't initiated by FDR. Rather, he greatly expanded the government spending the country into prosperity philosophy, an idea that seems to prevail in some among both of our ruling parties.

Mellon was a remarkable leader. He was later prosecuted and exonerated in two shameful tax trials that were regarded as political prosecutions that were a nasty joke. Even a hostile Mellon biographer, David Cannadine, who said he would have opposed Mellon's tax cutting policy, concedes Mellon was incredibly honest in his tax filings. He deliberately didn't claim certain deductions, Cannadine writes.

Nevertheless, Mellon, whose art collection was generously donated to the National Gallery, died before the exoneration of the second trial. FDR, later asked about the trial results, deviously answered that he was still waiting for a report from his attorney general. He pretended he had no idea what had happened to the controversial Mellon, a symbol of the low tax policies once popular in America. Mellon was exonerated and FDR must have known it but pulled a Jay Insley (When problems broke out in downtown Seattle in 2020, Insley, the governor of the state, initially claimed he knew nothing about them).

How was FDR doing with his attempts to restore prosperity by continuing and expanding the Hoover stimulus approach?

The Wrong Way to Escape a Depression---The Failure of the Hoover/FDR Stimulus

Under Hoover, and later FDR, the painful depression would go for more than a decade. Some defenders of various stimulus approaches concede the FDR policies didn't work; that prosperity was never restored.

What is the defense for these failed policies?

The same as today after every new round of big spending: The stimulus wasn't big enough. If it had been bigger, it would have worked, advocates said then and today. It's the drunk's rationale: Just give me one more drink and everything will be fine. But clearly, the most candid of FDR's supporters concede that, unlike under Harding's classical liberal measures, prosperity was never achieved though Roosevelt's policies of stimulus and market interventions.

"At no point during the 1930s did unemployment go below 14 percent," writes Jim Powell in "FDR's Folly." Median unemployment between 1934 and 1940 was 17.2 percent. "Even in 1941, amidst the military buildup for World War II, 9.9 percent of American workers were unemployed. Living standards remained depressed until after the war," Powell adds.

What happened after World War II?

The lessons of 1920-21 were partly applied. There was a tax cut. The economy started to recover.

The Choice Before Us

So what is to be the best way of climbing out of economic disaster?

A tax cut, says economist and Reagan/Trump adviser Arthur Laffer, "is much more effective in re-generating the economy that the government spending more money to stimulate the economy."

Indeed. History proves what is the right course. So Americans must answer these questions.

More stimulus and still more government spending, which is the Keynes/Hoover/FDR/Pelosi approach?

Or is to be the once traditional methods employed by presidents as varied Harding, Coolidge, Grover Cleveland, Ronald Reagan, Trump, Kennedy and Martin Van Buren.

These presidents from different centuries and parties showed one thing: They all faced economic disasters and all opted to let market forces operate. And in the case of Harding, Coolidge, Trump, Reagan and Kennedy they used tax cuts—more economic liberty for Americans—as a way to speed up the recovery process.

Tens of millions of Americans are hoping today's leaders will re-discover the old, hopefully not forgotten, methods of liberty.

These methods of liberty include each American employing thrift and spending discipline to achieve financial independence. They are also the principles of this book.

Gregory Bresiger, a longtime business writer with the New York Post Sunday Business section and Financial Advisor Magazine, is the author of a history of Social Security, "The Revolution of 1935." It is available at Mises.org. He also worked as a reporter and editor for Traders Magazine for 15 years and before that Financial Planning Magazine.

www.ingramcontent.com/pod-product-compliance
Lightning Source LLC
Chambersburg PA
CBHW071539200326
41519CB00021BB/6545